WHAT TO DO IN YOUR TEENAGE

HELPING YOU TO LIVE DIFFERENT

SOUMYARANJAN PANDA

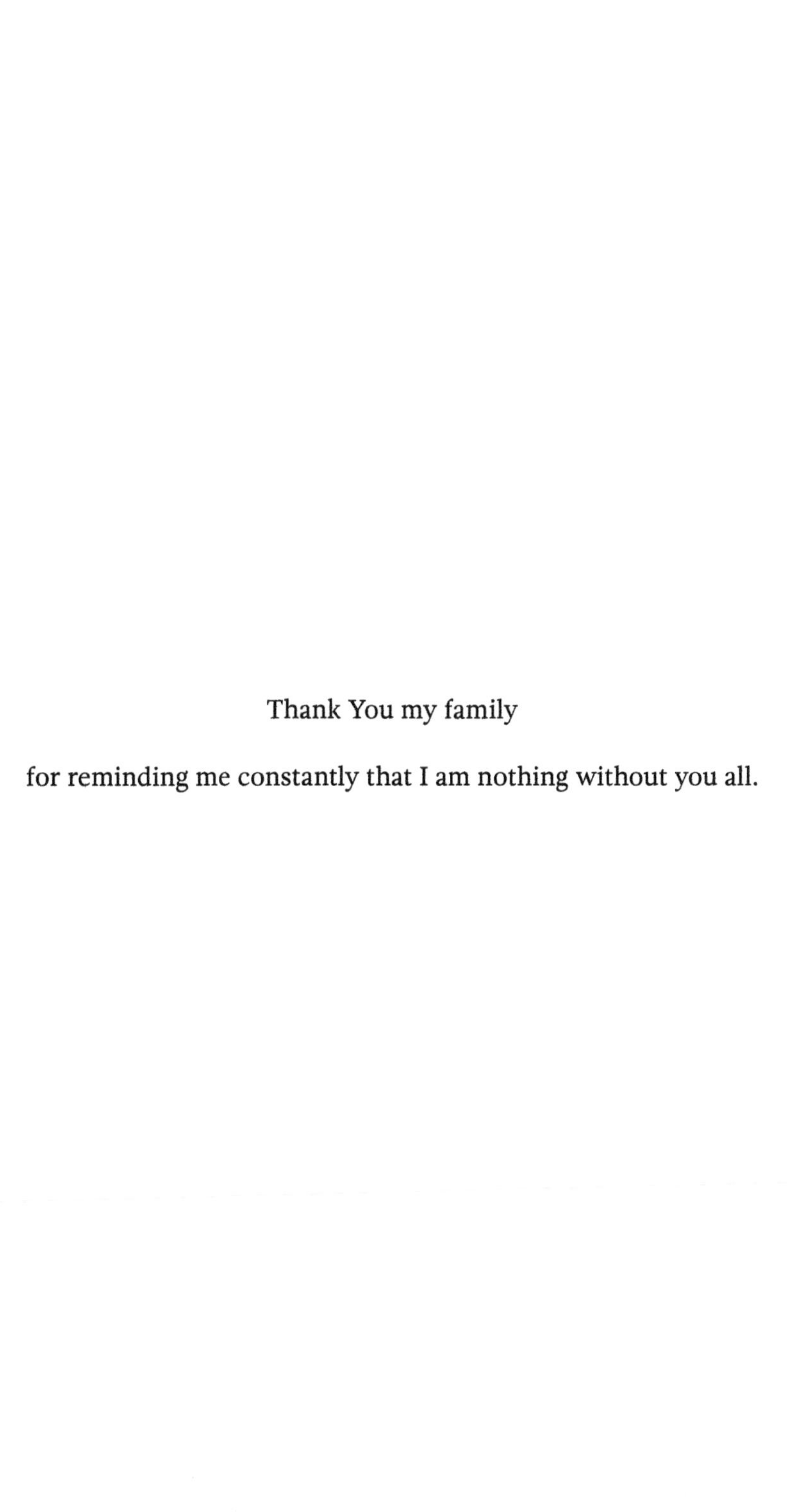

Thank You my family

for reminding me constantly that I am nothing without you all.

Contents

Contents

Contents

Foreword

Rugrats had a character who is 4-5 years old and she said to her friends that she got responsibilities and now she can't have fun and she can't play games with her friends. Even a small kid can think of it that responsibilities make you aware of your actions and let you know what to do and what to not. When I argue with my parents I make fake arguments and think these are natural but soon I realized that I am making a fool of myself and playing like a kid with my future and decided to end up these all things and to let other teenagers know about it.

Preface

Going to make you aware of your duties and help you with them. This book comprises 45 chapters that will help every teenager to build a perfect life. Real-life stories, Quotes, saying famous personalities, help others to motivate themselves, and the book is full of these things. People from different fields have different ideas on the same topic which will help you to decide which is better for you to make a decision.

Acknowledgements

Thank you to my readers who had chosen this book and letting me realize that I haven't wasted my time and ink, it is worthfull to someone.

Prologue

Congratulation, You took your first step toward the change in your life and now you have to follow the things mentioned in it to take your life to next level.

CHAPTER ONE

4 Things Successful Individuals Truly Do Before Bed

Day comes and dusks. Consistently we awaken with some new expectation for what's to come. Consistently we rest lamenting about the things that went poorly today. Consistently, we make guarantee to ourselves to work on something for a superior life. Notwithstanding, as day begins we just lose all sense of direction in day by day exercises.

We are doing same things again and expecting a superior life. On the off chance that we do same things consistently, how might we assume to get distinctive outcome? Achievement doesn't come for the time being. It requires consistent exertion and enhancements.

How might we follow that where we are going throughout everyday life? How might we assume responsibility for our life and get what we need?

Once more, the appropriate response is to do minimal consistently. Dissect yourself and help yourself the genuine reason to remember your life before you hitting the sack each day. Assuming you need to advance beyond swarm, figure out how to make basically slight upgrades in every day life.

The Importance of every day Self Evaluation:

Regardless is your fantasy, you as of now have some potential and abilities to accomplish them. In any case, regardless of how skilled you will be, you need to make a few moves. Assess yourself toward the day's end and investigate the activities that you made or that you ought to have made.

Do you assess yourself toward the finish of consistently? Do you set aside effort to help yourself the reason to remember your life? Do you snatch exercises from botches you are making each day?

You can't change everything in a solitary day. You need to gain ground each day. Make it a propensity. Effective individuals continually monitor their advancement and continue to learn for the duration of their life.

Check ordinary where are you going. You can assume responsibility for your life on the off chance that you can save 10 minutes for yourself before rest. Get some an ideal opportunity to check whether you accomplished something distinctively today than yesterday. Release us through the couple of significant things prior to having a tranquil rest:

4 Things Successful individuals do before Bed:

1.Understand the reason for your life: What are your fantasies? What is the reason for your living in this universe? Before you rest, envision your life. Have you effectively draw nearer to your objective today?

Make a stride. What parts of your life ask upgrades? It very well may be your vocation, connections, business, money or wellbeing. Get your drawn out objectives, plan for it and do it every day.

In case you are trusting that additional time will begin dealing with your fantasies, you won't ever get it. There will be no time when all that appears to consummate. It is vital for make one-stride ahead consistently. Little endeavors made regular transforms into large accomplishments.

2.Gain from botches: Everyone commit errors however not every person gain from it. It is human inclination to do exactly the same things ordinarily to keep away from the aggravation of un-safe place. By the day's end, close your eyes and check what has turned out badly today. What botch you have committed and do you make this error continually?

It very well may be starting off late consistently. It very well may be your unforgiving expressions of outrage with your relatives. It very well may be having issue while managing customer or director. Distinguish the space of progress. Until, you don't know about your mix-ups there is no possibility to dispose of them.

3.Celebrate and Give compensations to yourself: An insightful man realizes how to live each day. When second goes, it won't ever returned. Contemplate your prior day rest. Have you appreciated? Or then again you were too occupied to even consider discovering bliss minutes? Commend every little accomplishment and offer awards to yourself consistently.

Give yourself a congratulatory gesture for whatever great you have done today. Whatever you do, you accomplish for satisfaction. Hence, partake in each and every day of your life.

4.Release it: Last however not the least, let your brain be serene before rest. There is no utilization of lamenting for whatever happened today. When you distinguish and gain from botches, just let it proceed to pardon your-self.

Do you contemplate individuals who treated you terrible today? Mahatma Gandhi said, "The feeble can never pardon. Pardoning is the trait of the solid". Acknowledge as they are. Excuse them and move on.Do not offer space to feelings of spite, retribution and contempt to you. By pondering them, you essentially squander your energy on some unacceptable things. As you actually have a great deal to achieve in your life, why not to utilize your energy carefully on significant things.

CHAPTER TWO

HOW LONG WE WASTE DOING REST : 1

After the day by day feverish timetable, we frequently sit back before TV or rests on the bed and do rest. This is the manner by which we went through hours without accomplishing something useful. It is good to do rest and unwind for some time however the inquiry is how a lot.

Now and again we become apathetic and burn through a great deal within recent memory sitting idle. As Bruce Lee said, "In the event that you love life, don't sit around idly, for time is the thing that life is comprised of."

Do we truly require rest?

I mean it isn't care for 20 or 50 years prior, where the greater part of the normal work incorporates the actual exertion. In the past the greater part of individuals went through entire day doing a ton of work by their body rather than machines.

Do you burn through you actual effort the entire day? In the event that indeed, you should look for actual rest. On the off chance that you sit the entire day in an agreeable seat doing your paper/PC work, your body is as of now in actual solace.

Today the greater part of us sit before the PC or robotized machine and utilize our brain power as opposed to actual force. We are not truly extremely dynamic. Then, at that point what is the motivation behind your rest: to offer rest to mind right? You as of now have a major window as a rest time for that. Accordingly, utilize your get-togethers/work hours to accomplish something useful for you.

Why not to spent your vacation doing rest:

While I am discussing rest, I intended to be sitting or rests inactive at home or staring at the TV/News constantly. There is not all that much on the off chance that you go on an outing around the nation or get out for some diversion.

In any case, in case you are at home during your days off, get the chance to utilize that time. The second that we are passing won't ever returned. Accomplish something beneficial for your life.

We ought to hold onto every day. So it is possible that we ought to partake in our life or improving our life.

Why Politicians/Actors/Businessman doesn't rest?

You realize that they accomplish more work than you do. They merit more rest than you do. Obviously, they have more solace throughout everyday life. All things considered, the majority of them don't rest 7 hours per day.

What make all the difference for them: they like what they do. They are following their fantasies. They work day and night to get best in whatever they do. On the off chance that you hold similar enthusiasm for your fantasies and life, you won't ever really like to rest while you have something essential to do. Be energetic.

Why, we feel tired constantly?

There are many reasons. For instance, frequently we undermine our vocation as far as cash instead of premium.

We frequently see a lifelong where there is monetary development. Then, at that point we work all day regardless of whether we don't care for it. As you are detesting doing it, you will feel bore and power your psyche to take care of job that even you don't care for.

At the point when we do things that we don't care for, we watch out for apathetic on it. You will say that your brain isn't working. You feel tired soon and afterward request rest.

Reveal to me a certain something. In case you are playing an indoor game with your companion the entire day, will you feel tired? No. You might want to play one more round. Since your think that its intriguing. Make your work and life intriguing and you won't ever have to take rest.

CHAPTER THREE

How long we Waste doing Rest : 2

It is okay to take rest yet what amount?

For probably the first time, let us guess that you have done a ton of bookkeeping/paper/office work. You feel like your psyche is getting substantial and you need rest. Presently reveal to me how much rest will fill you with energy that you feel revived once more.

Is it accurate to say that one is hour works? Regularly we see that once we get along with bed, we would prefer not to get up. We need to sit or rests half more hour. Regardless of the amount we rest, we need to accomplish more. Why? Since this rest won't ever work. You are attempting to offer rest to your psyche however it is getting stressing over previous happenings or forthcoming difficulties.

For a brain, a 5-minute sitting peacefully is sufficient to unwind whenever done appropriately. In any case, we are regularly overpowered with negative musings today that it never resists the urge to panic. Extraordinary compared to other approaches to loosen up your brain is Meditation.

Where are you going in Life?

We regularly went through years to take training and degrees, however never invested energy to consider our life. How long you extra to ponder yourself? The amount you know about the course of your life. Is it going in right manner?

On the off chance that you feel that you are following your life objectives and dreams, sluggishness and sleepiness won't discover any spot in your life. In any case, in case you are stuck some place in your own life, profession or connections, you will consistently feel like you are missing something throughout everyday life.

What to do as opposed to doing Rest:

It is good to figure out an ideal opportunity for amusement. What is the utilization of living in case you are hating your life? Nonetheless, never at any point burn through your time sitting idle. Toward the finish of the life, will you recollect your season of rest or additional rest?

There ought to be no lament in future about doing nothing previously. Invest your lay energy chipping away at yourself, your relationship, your vocation and your fantasies. On the off chance that you make one good stride in any part of your life, trust me you won't feel the need of having rest. Subsequently, Do not Rest, Do your Best.

How we burn through our time:

Allow us to assume you have 2-3 hours time after office. You will invest some energy sitting in front of the TV/Movies/ Entertainment. A portion of that time, you will converse with your companions on friendly destinations or tattle with your mates/ relatives. Presently it is 30 minutes left for supper. You will imagine that this ought to be the ideal opportunity for rest.

Presently advise me, what was that tattle or amusement? Your amusement has effectively loosened up your psyche and you needn't bother with rest any longer.

On the off chance that you actually need, sit in the quietness for 5 minutes or talk decidedly to yourself. Then, at that point get up and utilize that passed on half hour to coordinate your life. Perceive how your life going on and which life needs your work to be ideal.

As I previously said, in the event that you take even one small (extra) good advance, you will feel confident and upbeat. Your will get yourself ready for business and edified.

Convert your Rest into Achievement:

For instance, on the off chance that you have making progress toward a superior profession life. Do minimal ordinarily to sharp your ability. Throughout the time, you will be prepared to make a lifelong move. In case you are experiencing issues seeing someone, work on it.

On the off chance that you imagine that, any of your propensity is upsetting you from getting achievement. For what reason don't you chip away at it? It might require little exertion at first, yet when you recognize the distinction in your life, you will be exceptionally cheerful. It will help you in different parts of your life also.

Frequently we disparage the force of ourselves to manage these life challenges. Since we don't make any stride.

On the off chance that you feel that life gives you additional time for these things, you are making numb-skull of yourself. You need to utilize your time. You need to figure out your time. Make your ordinary countable.

No one is great. It is okay gaining from other people who are acceptable in those spaces. Investigate books, individuals and different sources where you can learn. Continue to work on yourself, life will be delightful.

CHAPTER FOUR

Instructions to Form a New Habit Successfully

It is the start of the year. Everybody is discussing goals. We regularly choose to leave the negative propensities that debase the nature of our life. Moreover, we need to shape new propensities that can lead us to a superior life.

Significance of Making New Habits:

Framing another propensity is consistently a fresh start to personal development. The more you try different things with life, the better your life will be. In any case, for the most part our new propensity last just for few days or weeks. This is interesting however at times we don't begin.

It is nice to attempt again and never stopping something in view of disappointment. We should to gain from previous mishaps and improve sometime later.

Each time you make a goal or propensity, you are reminding yourself an objective. You can't gain ground without having these objectives. Consequently, consistently continue to make progress toward a superior self. On the off chance that you improve yourself, the world around your look better consequently.

Why Habit Fails:

Consistently I set up New Year goals and choose to frame new propensities. At times I succeed while I come up short at not many things. On the off chance that I look at those fizzled and effective goals, I can see the distinction.

Achievement principally associated with your cravings and interest. On the off chance that you really need to accomplish something and it satisfy you, you will do it at any expense.

Framing another propensity likewise requires a predictable exertion. Frequently we anticipate moment result. At the point when we don't get it, we lost energy. We will in general stall. We concoct rationalization, for example, we are not getting sufficient opportunity.

See at the higher perspective while making another propensity. It might require some investment at first however the outcome could change the remainder of your life. You need to prepare for putting forth additional attempt to get a bonus throughout everyday life.

Step by step instructions to Form a Habit Successfully:

Our reasoning and conviction massively affects the accomplishment of shaping another propensity. You might have question on a few, on which you fizzled before.

When you settle your New Year goals or any propensity, sit quiet for few moments. Then, at that point, in the event that you think sanely, you definitely know which of them will succeed.

Thusly, pause for a moment before chipping away at a similar propensity as last year. In the first place, check why you need to do this. Then, at that point see, what you will do another way this chance to make it effective.

Here are a few focuses that assist us with Forming a New Habit Successfully:

1.Do just assuming you need to do: The genuine and enduring inspiration comes from the inside. Assume you are intrigued with somebody and chose to do comparable this year. It very well may be "fast found and simple lost" inspiration. Check in the event that you truly need to do it for yourself or you need to show the world. Your propensity will last on the off chance that you have more spotlight on Internal Rewards instead of External Rewards.

2.Accept that you can do it: If you are beginning something with question, it will lead you to disappointment. In the first place, give yourself enough motivations to legitimize why you can do it. Then, at that point start it. Your energy of accomplishment ought to be higher than your feeling of dread toward disappointment. Have confidence in yourself and you are most of the way there.

3.Assume liability of disappointment: We frequently attempt new things told by somebody renowned or ace. Some of the time, we do this is on the grounds that referenced in a book. In the event that we succeed, we offer credit to ourselves. In any case, we accept that in the event that we fizzle, it is their disappointment. No.Take obligation of your disappointment in case it isn't working for you. You know there are numerous who got achievement utilizing same recipes. When you get this, you will toss your best exertion and there will be shocking outcomes.

4.Never quit in the Middle: I generally encountered that when you need to begin something, obscure and unsure circumstances reaches stop you. Then again, when you are doing admirably with your new propensity or goal, something comes to break the example. Keep in mind:

It is okay in the event that you were unable to do it for few days. Never let this interruptions/hole function as a pardon to stops you in your excursion. Continue onward.

5.Have persistence: Most of the time the effect of our propensities are not moment. For instance, you have surrendered outrage yet it doesn't appear a lot of effect on your relationship. Might be you have mastered another expertise, yet you can't utilize it anyplace yet.Have tolerance. Your work will have an effect at the ideal opportunity. As Paulo Coelho said, "Nothing on the planet is at any point totally off-base. Indeed, even a halted clock is correct double a day."

Today, we care our family to such an extent. We buckle down for our vocation. We put forth an attempt to make ourselves monetarily solid. Nonetheless, we neglect to deal with internal identity. We are living in the torment each day on account of our propensities. Is it true that you are prepared to roll out an improvement?

Allow us to vow to chip away at ourselves this year. Allow us to check what propensities clashing with your bliss. Allow us to deal with our body and psyche. Allow us to live a sound, serene and cheerful life.

CHAPTER FIVE

Contemplation: A Way to interface with God

Contemplation works on our physical just as psychological wellness. It builds our center, guarantees true serenity and makes you innovative.

There are unlimited advantages of contemplation. Alongside these advantages, it is an amazing method to interface with God. Today, we will perceive how reflection works for us as a scaffold to make an association with god.

Why we need to associate with God:

Regardless of whether today science has arrived at moon, we don't have every one of the appropriate responses. We can see bewildering improvements and unbelievable machines surrounding us. Current innovation has worked on our life to such an extent. Still we feel vacancy inside.

Who can fill that void?

Undoubtedly, our family, companions and associates make our life dynamic. Still we feel the absence of fulfillment at various occasions throughout everyday life. There is an extreme fulfillment, when we interface with God. He is the preeminent force. In any event, when nothing works for us, his endowments work.

Commonly throughout everyday life, we face questions that no one appears to know answers. Everybody has alternate point of view yet no one appears to be persuading. Not many inquiries must be replied by God.

On the off chance that we get associate with divine force, He can show us right bearing. For that, make an individual relationship with God, so you can converse with Him straightforwardly.

What's your opinion on the various strategies to make an association with God?

Distinctive approaches to associate with God:

We follow various ways to interface with God. We visit to blessed spots. We do conventional petitions. We serenade mantras. We follow certain custom like contribution water to sun and some more.

Various individuals put stock in an unexpected way. What we need to check is the way compelling our direction is. What is the utilization of doing supplication on the off chance that you don't feel associated with God? The majority of these profound practices have become a piece of our life yet we are missing soul in them.

The greater part of the customary strategies functions as an uneven correspondence. Frequently, we are asking God for the things however don't attempt to hear his answers. A solid association requires two-sided correspondence.

We request that God get us our objective. We as a whole need instant things from God. We need to comprehend that God can show us way and we need to walk that way. Consequently, rather than objective, request bearing.

How lovely it is, on the off chance that you can have a discussion with God. Indeed, you can converse with god. Maybe than basically rehash a similar mantra/petition each day, converse with him. He can address the entirety of your inquiries.

For that, you need to make a relationship with God. What sort of relationship you need to settle on is absolutely your decision.

Reflection: A Way to Connect with God:

Intervention is extraordinary compared to other approaches to interface with God.

By Mediation, you can make an individual relationship with God. In any connections what do you do? You should have something to share. You have a few inquiries to pose. Indeed, you may very well need to make proper acquaintance. You can set up your discussion in your manner.

There is no compelling reason to confound the things. Here are straightforward advances you can follow to associate with God:

1.Track down a tranquil spot.

2.Close your eyes assuming you need.

3.You will feel the combination of musings running to you. Your psyche is as yet contemplating your day by day exercises. Your emphasis is as yet on the thing is circumventing you.

4.Acknowledge for what it's worth. Simply unwind and try to avoid panicking inside. Request each from your idea to disappear for some time. Trust me they can pay attention to you.

5.Presently, you are prepared to have a discussion with God.

6.Consider him to be a state of light before you. Consider him to be your dad or companion. Picture him in any capacity you can most interface.

7.Presently converse with him. Offer what you got. Ask what you need.

8.Pay attention to him with soul and you will find every one of the solutions. You will discover him addressing a portion of the inquiries right away. A portion of your inquiries will discover answers by means of another source while working for the duration of the day.

9.Request that he give you power in case you are feeling frail to adapt up to things.

10.Envision beams of light coming into you. You will feel incredible and solid.

11.Express profound gratitude to God and open your eyes. You can feel the divine nature.

Examination yourself and see the distinction. As Swami Sivananda said, "Reflection is excruciating before all else however it gives undying Bliss and preeminent satisfaction eventually."

Building a Strong Relationship with God:

At first, it might set aside effort to get interface. It is about how much confidence you have in God. You can change the above approach in your manner.

When an association is set up, your relationship will get more grounded with the time.

When you have solid and cozy relationship, you even don't have to sit inactive to interface with God. You can converse with him whenever anyplace. You can converse with him in the transport, train or swarmed places. Accept and witness wonders.

CHAPTER SIX

Be Flexible like Water

Do you need a protected occupation for rest of your life? Do you focus on hazard free business? Would you like to carry on with a steady life? We as a whole need to have an existence with no battle by any stretch of the imagination. See your previous existence and advise me on the off chance that you at any point discovered an individual who has done that?

Assuming you need to see yourself at a position where everything is good, you would not have the option to discover it in the whole your life. Regardless of how rich and favored an individual is, there would be a few difficulties in their day to day existence. We don't understand however more often than not challenges are just a type of progress.

Things continue to change. You will discovered something new to manage for the duration of your life. Assuming you need to get moving, you need to figure out how to adjust those progressions and difficulties. You can't generally change conditions. Notwithstanding, you can figure out how to live with optimistic mood in any circumstance.

Our brain is incredible to such an extent that it can generally discover a way. We ought to be available to change the perspective. A definitive objective of our life is to continue to push ahead with better decisions. As Alison Gopnik said, "The cerebrum is exceptionally organized, yet it is likewise amazingly adaptable. It's anything but a clean canvas, however it isn't written in stone, all things considered."

Allow us to perceive how to be adaptable to adapt up to life changes.

Change is Constant:

The lone consistent thing in life is change. Regardless of how huge organization you are functioning for, you will confront new liabilities with the time. You have a glad family, however you will see changes in customs while your children are developing. Your organization is overwhelming in the business; you will make contests with the time.

Not all progressions are deterrents. The majority of these hindrances basically push you out of your agreeable zone. It is fundamental to escape your agreeable zone to continue to move with life. All life resembles an excursion. You generally have degree to turn out to be superior to what you as of now are. These life changes carry freedoms to outwit you.

Be Flexible like Water:

Have you perceived how water streams? Undoubtedly, you know. Regardless comes into the way of water, it makes its own particular manner. Be adaptable like water. You can't generally pick your life occasions, however you can generally be adaptable to change your methodology according to your conditions.

At the point when the water of waterway streams, it experiences obstructions like slopes, stones and rocks and route. In the first place, it attempts to remove them from his way with its force of reach. Nonetheless, if water doesn't ready to discard it, it doesn't stop there. It changes himself toward another path. This is the adaptability of water.

Stream like Water:

Stream like water while managing troubles. Try not to be so inflexible to change your methodology. It is a great idea to be unmistakable about your life objectives yet be adaptable with your methodology. In the event that one way isn't getting you there, attempt another. Continue onward and continue to stream.

Take another model. At the point when the tempest strikes wilderness, not all trees endure similarly. The trees that realize how to twist stay alive while storm separates the unbending ones. I might want to wind up this article with a decent statement about adaptability.

CHAPTER SEVEN

Joy can be Found, even in the Darkest of Times

The "Up" and "Down" are fundamental piece of life as day and night. We have profound established faith to us that in case everything is acceptable, I would be glad. This isn't accurate. You are the proprietor of your joy button. You can squeeze this catch whenever to be content.

In "Harry Potter and the Prisoner of Azkaban", a person Albus Dumbledore says a magnificent line regarding bliss:

"Joy can be found, even in the haziest of times, on the off chance that one just makes sure to turn on the light."

This one line by Steven Kloves (screenplay) says all regarding bliss. We can figure out how to be content in any condition in the event that we recollect that we own our joy. Sadly, a large portion of us gave this power to individuals and conditions to make us cheerful and dismal.

Never Waste a day without Happiness:

How regularly you wound up in the haziness of life. Do you recall around then to turn on the light? Life is spending step by step and we are spending these days without truly getting a charge out of it. A large portion of us are really not carrying on with life, yet passing life.

Review the times of your last month. The amount you delighted in it. What number of bliss minutes were there? In case you can't discover enough, you are not living enough. Quit squandering your days, quit squandering your life.

There are so many days has been squandered expecting a superior tomorrow. Let us not squander one more day and figure out how to live cheerfully in any condition.

Offer it a Reprieve to the Problems:

Living on a cheap food, our age needs everything quick. We need handy solution for everything. We need alternate ways to the objective. On the off chance that we didn't get that, we revile fortune and ourselves. We begin encountering torment, stress or dejection.

Since one thing isn't working for you, don't invest all your energy crying about it. Leave it for some time and spotlight on different things. On the off chance that you don't appear to discover an answer, offer it a reprieve.

For a model, in case you are not finding a nice line of work, continue to get ready and have a break between. In the event that a relationship doesn't working for you, enjoy a reprieve agonizing over it. On the off chance that your conference didn't go true to form, don't destroy your rest of the day and enjoy a reprieve.

Remember to press your Happiness button

During break, remember to press your satisfaction button. There could be distinctive type of bliss button for everybody. Play your #1 music track for some time. Proceed to have a stroll for some time. Peruse a most recent novel or something. Go for a film or play your number one game.

At the point when you turned on your joy, it revives and supports your psyche's force. You will feel all the more impressive to manage the conditions. Enormous issues appear to be nearly nothing. You become acquainted with that it is only the issue of time and all that will be okay.

Where to discover satisfaction:

Joy is consistently around us. We continue to see wrong spot frequently. We anticipate it from others and on the off chance that we didn't get, we expect that we didn't merit it.

Satisfaction is now there within you. You simply need to encounter it. You can feel it in the easily overlooked details. Nonetheless, on the off chance that you would prefer not to be content, it's not possible for anyone to make you. It is forever your choice to be content.

One satisfaction second prompts more bliss:

Satisfaction prompts bliss and trouble make misery. It streams like a waterway, when you direct it. Assume, one thing turned out badly and it ruins your minutes. Presently in the event that you neglect to press your bliss button for long time, it will ruin your entire day.

Likewise, scarcely any bliss minutes can prompts flood of satisfaction. Allow us to make some joy toward the beginning of the day and you will be glad and charmed entire day.

Another approach to make joy is to fulfill others. Give joy and you will encounter the joy and happiness. Spread joy and grin around you. The more you give, the more it returns to you.

There isn't fortunate or unfortunate time for joy. You can generally discover it. Regardless of how much haziness is there, one flame is barely enough to spread light. Continuously make sure to fire your joy light throughout everyday life.

CHAPTER EIGHT

Your Responsibility is to Create Joy in Pain

Why it happens that regardless of the amount we plan, life takes turn and we wind up in torment? This is the idea of life. It is our obligation to discover light in the haziness.

Life brings difficulties at each phase of life. What we can do is, first acknowledge the negative shades of life and quit battling with them. See brilliant side of everything and keep yourself charmed.

Do you believe that one day the entirety of your issues will get settled and you will be glad for eternity? Disregard it. It is never going to occur. You need to figure out how to be content alongside every one of the difficulties life brings you.

As Milton Erickson said, "Life will bring you torment without help from anyone else. Your obligation is to make euphoria."

Allow us to perceive how to Create Joy in Pain:

Try not to trust that Result will Enjoy:

I can see individuals around me make a solid effort to create the ideal outcome. They imagine that once they achieve this, they would be cheerful and figure out how to appreciate. When they achieve it, they got another task. This is life.

On the off chance that you delay your bliss for some other time, it won't ever come. Appreciate while dealing with every day exercises. You have effectively heard it ordinarily that Life is an excursion. In the event that you can't partake in your excursion, objective won't give you much to appreciate. In the event that you realize how to appreciate venture, you realize how to appreciate life.

Remember about Happiness:

Life is a ceaseless mission. We can't save our joy for retirement. When, you will fail to remember what bliss is.

Appreciate being Alive.

When did last time you awaken and expressed profound gratitude to god for another exquisite day. You can improve the worth of your day by paying appreciation each day. Be glad that you have given one more day. Appreciate being alive.

Today is another day:

Consistently when you awaken advise yourself that today is the new day. Disregard all the aggravation you had on yesterday. Today brings new freedoms.

Be that as it may, actually we live previously. We frequently bring agony of past into today and ruin our opportunity to embrace current circumstances. For what reason don't you do the new? Feel the excellence of today and live it completely.

Pick joy:

Joy is a choice. In the event that you can decide to be content, you can be cheerful at the present time. On the off chance that you set conditions to be content, they won't ever get satisfy. Regardless of whether you met conditions, your satisfaction would not last as conditions continue to change.

The greater part of us purchase material things to fulfill us. These things can bring us solace however not bliss. Solace can give us satisfaction to some time, yet inside bliss is endless joy. Feel the delight within you.

Care Happiness:

In the event that you care for your satisfaction, bliss deals with you. Discover the exercises that are near your spirits. Play like a child. Being a grown-up never intended to genuine 24 hours. Being an expert never intended to discover bliss just in ends of the week. Regardless of how bustling you are, do seemingly insignificant details that you love. Care for yourself.

Offer joy:

Do you share joy? It doesn't require some investment. Your one grin can share joy around you. Spread the aroma of joy with your environmental elements. As Mother Teresa said, "Let nobody at any point come to you without leaving better and more joyful."

Just getting by can be a struggle for the individuals who treat themselves as a survivor of life. Life is a good time for the individuals who relax and discover minutes to chuckle each day. Regardless concerns you have, you can in any case discover joy around you. In the event that you realize how to discover it, your issues will begin abhorring you and go straight away.

Keep in mind: This second is life. You won't get your minutes back. Live however much you can at this time. A savvy realizes how to praise the straightforward delights every day with the goal that you can partake in your life ride. Be shrewd; be glad.

CHAPTER NINE

INSTRUCTIONS TO STAY AWAY FROM 9 THINGS THAT STEAL YOUR JOY

There are two reasons that get us far from our bliss:

One is that we don't zero in on seemingly insignificant details that can satisfy us. Second, we center around easily overlooked details that don't actually matter throughout everyday life except takes our joy.

Why we can't be cheerful every one of the 24 hours? Since, we have effectively concluded that we can't go on without stress and pressure. We have made distress and melancholy our piece of every day life. The tallness is that you can spend entire day without bliss yet you can't track down an entire day without some concern.

We are striving to get more things ordinary yet the degree of bliss getting down. Wouldn't you say that we were more joyful as a youngster when we don't had large things?

All our day we watch out for other people. What others are doing? Why they are doing as such? Then, at that point we say they are the explanation that you are upset.

We revile others as well as ourselves. We continue to think what we have done previously. We continue to stress what to do later on.

Just saying that we don't actually appreciate what is acceptable in the present. We let not many things (underlined) takes our joy for the duration of the day. Tell us how we ought not deal with carry on with a glad life.

Here, 9 things that Steal your Joy and how to keep away from them:

Try not to Compare yourself with others:

From adolescence, we begin looking at things we get. We contrast it and our sibling, sisters and companions. That is the point we hold a conviction that we will be glad when we have more than what others have.

Indeed, even once in a while, we are cheerful in light of the fact that others are in torment. That way you can see that your joy is thoroughly relies upon others. Quit doing examination. Be glad since you got something. Not on the grounds that you got something, better than others.

Try not to Brood over your Past Mistakes:

Do you pain over your previous mishaps. Regularly we burn through a lot of effort on the past. You will say that it isn't so natural to fail to remember those things. Keep in mind, simple or troublesome: it is a decision at any rate.

We can pick our contemplations. Advise yourself in case it merits pondering that. Will thinking will fix it. No, it can't. Whatever happened has given you some exercise. Be glad for that learning and go on.

Try not to Judge an individual by their appearance:

They say that first articulation is last articulation. That can be valid in case somebody is visiting for a meeting or conference. Nonetheless, with regards to pick your companions, take as much time as is needed.

Try not to pass judgment on individuals by means of their actual appearance and garments. You can't generally pass judgment flippantly.

Try not to Expect a lot from others:

"I have worked on something for other people. Consequently, he ought to do that for me also." What is that: a relationship or business? Leave them alone allowed to do what they need. Try not to anticipate that others should do the manner in which you need without fail. Expect less and you don't wind up hurt any longer.

Try not to Postpone your bliss:

Try not to design everything for retirement. Today is an ideal opportunity to appreciate life. It is great to get ready for future yet not at the expense of today. Discover minutes to commend occasionally. At the deathbed, you won't be as glad for you have accomplished as opposed to what you appreciated.

Try not to hold Grudges:

Try not to hold other's mix-ups to you for long time. It will just eat your joy time by time. Simply neglect and excuse. Also, recall that it isn't for him however for the better of you.

Try not to Wait for the ideal second:

Do you have dreams? Try not to trust that ideal time and conditions will start. Wonderful opportunity won't ever come. When you begin dealing with your fantasy, you appreciate all that you do. Else, you will think twice about it later that why you have not begun it before.

Remember to be grateful for what you have:

Remember to appreciate what you like. Like the excellence around you. Tell your family the amount you love them. Paying appreciation expands the worth of individuals and things in our day to day existence. It fulfills others which thus satisfies you too.

Try not to stress over things that are outside your ability to control:

Do you contemplate whatever awful is occurring on the planet? Do you stress over things for them you can sit idle. Stress won't settle anything. Acknowledge the things that you can't handle and zero in on the part that you can handle.

Everybody has his own influence here. God has a superior arrangement for everybody. You simply center around your part.

Have your impact well and be cheerful. Try not to attempt to control everything in your life. It will obliterate your joy. Be adaptable like water and you will be glad constantly.

CHAPTER TEN

Do you Learn from Mistakes?

Error is a demonstration or judgment that is confused or wrong. However long we exist, we commit errors deliberately or unwittingly.

Oblivious Mistakes:

A few errors we made in view of the absence of information or experience. It very well may be determination of subjects or school in case you are an understudy. A youth can pick a profession that doesn't line up with his life reason. It very well may be a choice that caused misfortune in business in case you are a financial specialist.

Cognizant Mistakes:

There are not many mix-ups we rehash regular intentionally. We name it as a propensity or sluggishness. For a model: you realize that you will get discipline, if arriving behind schedule in school or office. Also, you are doing it consistently. That is cognizant error.

It is the point at which we stuck consistently in office work without taking any kind of action for it. It is the point at which you realize your relationship isn't working and you are hauling it at any rate. It is the point at which you squander a day accomplishing something incorrectly and rehash it following day too.

Why we commit Errors?

For our entire life we do explores different avenues regarding things. Some of the time it works and at times it doesn't. During these trials botches occurs. As Albert Einstein said, "An individual who never committed an attempted had a go at nothing new."

Misstep likewise happen in light of our thoughtlessness or absence of preparation. Disappointment is additionally treated as one's slip-up some of the time.

Mix-up doesn't mean Failure:

It isn't generally an error on the off chance that you fall flat at something. Now and again disappointment happens when we get things done interestingly to escape our usual range of familiarity. This is the means by which we learn. Make such analyses to push ahead throughout everyday life.

At the point when we take a stab at something new and come up short, we face a ton of analysis. It makes dread inside us and stops us to make next stride. Never be deterred from these slip-ups throughout everyday life.

"The best slip-up you can make in life is to be consistently dreading you will make one." ~ Elbert Hubbard, The Note Book, 1927

Never Quit. The Important is to gain from the missteps with the goal that you can improve sometime later.

Do you gain from Mistakes?

It is not difficult to commit errors however difficult to gain from them. This is the explanation we continue to rehash them. Each mix-up offers an exercise in case we are prepared to get it.

Check yourself. Rundown the things that you need to do another way yet rehash them consistently.

It very well may be a connected thing to your relationship. It harms when you battle with your friends and family. You realize that you have your a lot of slip-up. Then, at that point you choose to take care sometime later. Be that as it may, it happens again following day.

What did you gain from yesterday? You can't generally fault the other one. First ask yourself, did you accomplished something in an unexpected way?

Take another model: You are planning for any test or your next work change. In any case, you squander a day without taking any kind of action for it. You lament toward the day's end and rehash exactly the same thing following day. What have you realized?

Try not to give me pardon of propensity. You can generally get out from under a propensity by little practice each day in the event that you truly need to.

Gain from other's Mistakes also:

You can see individuals falling flat and prevailing around you. You more likely than not heard stories from your folks about the missteps they made in the course of their life. Keep your eyes open and gain from them.

Understand histories. Go to classes and get together. Peruse examples of overcoming adversity. They will stop for a minute method to follow and keep away from. You life is too short to even consider learning all by doing test yourself. Accordingly, gain from others too.

Committing errors isn't learning; it is remedying those mix-ups:

As it's been said, we gain from botches. Here, It is significant is to understand that we don't simply learn by committing errors yet amending those mix-ups.

We as a whole have flimsy spots. We as a whole commit errors. We recall the initial segment that slip-ups are important forever. The subsequent part is to address those missteps.

The vast majority of us commit another error in the wake of committing an error. We lament and sorrow over the misstep. We contemplate what turned out badly. By doing this we essentially sit around idly. You can't change what has occurred however can generally improve sometime later.

Basic strides to address Mistakes:

1.At the point when we come up short at something or something turns out badly: First thing is perceiving what turned out badly and why.

2.Until you discover your blame or perceive your mix-up, you can't fix or gain from it. Make a rundown of the disappointment factors in case they are many. Perceive the week focuses.

3.Regardless of whether it was another person's deficiency, see what can be done. Notwithstanding, it is smarter to initially zero in on your part.

4.Presently plan ventures for the remedy. In case it was the absence of data, set it up for the following time. In case it is absence of expertise, learn it.

5.In case there is some propensity you rehash each day, break the example by venturing out. Practice and work on yourself doing minimal consistently.

6.Continue learning and partake in your being a superior variant of yourself.

Consider errors to be a piece of life. Consider them to be an occasion from which you can generally learn something. They basically exist to make us solid with the time.

How delightful our life will be in the event that we quit lamenting the previous oversights and lay them down to fill in as a way for a superior future.

CHAPTER ELEVEN

TELL YOUR FAMILY YOU LOVE THEM

How regularly do you say, "I love you" to your beau, sweetheart or life partner. It sounds simple and self-evident. How frequently do you tell your family that you love them? Presently it sounds hard for the majority of us. Isn't that right?

Why we don't show our affection to our relatives? Above all, contemplate our folks, who raised us for quite a long time?

Do you adore them? Indeed!

Do you advise them? No!

We imagine that telling isn't significant in family since it is reasonable that we love them. Allow us to perceive how obvious it is.

Why Tell them:

Every one of our idea, word and activity either makes our breaks relationship. At the point when we don't care for something about our folks, we remember to grumble. The time has come to think whether we like them enough for every one of the beneficial things that they accomplish for us. Why it is significant?

At the point when we show our affection to family, it makes a layer of care around our friends and family. This layer secures our connections with regards to contrasts and misconstruing. Our customary love and care makes that "Adoration Layer" solid.

What do you think how solid your Love Layer is? Do you regularly share cherish and get things done for your family? If not yet, let them know now. It resembles adding to make a superior family and a superior world.

Why we ought not Hide our Love:

Everybody adores his family. Notwithstanding, everybody conceal these sentiments in the psyche. We frequently ended up absence of word or time to communicate our adoration. Why?

Allow us to see another perspective. Do you keep very when recognize their shortcomings?

Assume, your sibling broke ceramics in the kitchen or your mom has neglected to add salt in the supper. You immediately respond and grumble about that. Presently advise me, do you immediately appreciate also?

You realize that we don't think much prior to censuring them. Then, at that point, for what reason to think a great deal when there is an ideal opportunity to cherish them. Simply envision for some time your child or girl come to you and says, "Love you mother" or "Love you father". It sounds incredibly delightful and you feel total in this world.

Life is passing second by second. Might be tomorrow, there will be no time passed on to communicate your affection and care for them. Today is the time. Tell them.

There should be some forte of every one of your relative. The time has come to perceive and like that. Tell your sibling how great he is at sport. Say your sister that she cooks stunning. Other than that, let them realize that you are fortunate to have them.

Let's assume it more than you share on Social Media:

Keep going month on Women's day, I shared a post on Facebook. That wonderful post has pleasant words that accolade for my mom. Then, at that point an idea hit into my brain. Did I wish my mom "Cheerful Women's Day"? No. Indeed, even she didn't think about that day.

How tragic I thought. Notwithstanding, I did it later on that day and felt so great.

As an another take, we are lounging around feasting table with Smartphone close by and sharing status like "I love my folks" and so on Notwithstanding, we don't give any consideration to our mom who is setting us up food with such a lot of adoration.

That is the thing that a large portion of us are doing. We report our consideration for the friends and family to the world yet don't defy with one another. Allow us first to get genuine and afterward friendly. On the off chance that you truly love them, for what reason don't initially advise them prior to sharing it on Facebook/ Twitter.

On the off chance that we deal with these seemingly insignificant details, they can feed our connections. Is it accurate to say that you are prepared to do it now? Allow us to set a lovely assignment during the current week. Allow us to communicate our affection to every one of relative. Tell all of them that "I love you".

CHAPTER TWELVE

Might It Be Said That We Are Getting Ready Future at the Expense of Present? : 1

In this transitory and short life, we endeavor to make our future splendid. Nonetheless, deny embracing the here and now. The inquiry is; do we get a future that we expect? You can find that answer in your parent's life too.

Ask any parent in their 30s or 40s, in case they are happy with their life. Check whether they are truly partaking in their life consistently. Unquestionably, the appropriate response you will find that they are planning for their future and kids' vocation. Thusly, they didn't have the opportunity to ponder themselves today.

Regularly we set up our future at the expense of present and that future won't ever come.

How we plan for our future?

We as a whole know the significance of cash and subsequently successfully save a ton of it for what's to come. Interestingly, more often than not we do it at the expense of today. Here is the secret:

As of late, when I was voyaging Delhi metro, I saw a promotion for an exceptionally perceived emergency clinic around there. The banner recorded different administrations they offer alongside their high rates. I was believing that whatever we are saving today we are putting something aside for them.

Wouldn't you say so?

Get any relative and ponder their wellbeing today. Everybody appears to have some medical problem. The majority of them became sick once in a while. There will be rest issue with somebody. Some may have experiencing sorrow while some from diabetes. A few has low/hypertension while some are experiencing heart infections.

These sicknesses have become so normal today on account of our way of life. Since we are experts and work is love for us, we lack the capacity to deal with genuine self.

We don't have the opportunity to prepare good food, so depend on inexpensive food. There is no an ideal opportunity to do morning activity or contemplation. We sit in our workplaces entire day without doing any substantial active work. Then, at that point, we sit so long before the TV however don't have the opportunity to contemplate ourselves.

Regardless of whether our wellbeing appears all good, we don't live in introduce and thusly don't appear to be content. I accept that in case you are detesting your life, you are not carrying on with your life. That is likewise a typical infection today. It implies that you are essentially passing your present and trusting (really stressing) for a superior future.

What do you think we are doing today really?

In reality, we are completing two things simultaneously. We are setting up our body to experience later on and planning cash for its treatment too. Isn't it entertaining?

How we plan for our youngsters?

According to the vast majority of the guardians, they have devoted their life for their kids' schooling and vocation. They caused penances with their life to guarantee that their youngsters to have a superior future. The intension is awesome without a doubt. Notwithstanding, let us examine the existence cycle.

After a well-rounded schooling, young person goes into a great job. Presently as he remains at his feet and guardians expect that their youngster will do likewise for them. A kid just began partaking in his life and needed to do numerous things for him and his family too. Indeed, he will actually want to do it several years.

Simultaneously, he is entering in a similar stage. He is getting hitched. Presently he will have youngsters and more obligations. Cash never is by all accounts enough to manage the cost of all costs. He compromise with his wellbeing and dreams, just for their youngsters and a safe future.

He devotes rest of his life accomplishing for them with the assumption that one day they will satisfy their fantasies. Also, here is the manner by which parent's fantasies constrained on the kids (That is somewhat unique point). In any case, presently you may have a feeling that how this cycle proceeds.

Everybody feels that he has carried on with his life for other people. Then, at that point who carries on with his life really. It is smarter to carry on with your own life well first and others will do the equivalent naturally.

CHAPTER THIRTEEN

MIGHT IT BE SAID THAT WE ARE GETTING READY FUTURE AT THE EXPENSE OF PRESENT? : 2

Future arrangement never arrives at end:

In the event that we keep cash on the highest point of everything, we are never going to be fulfilled.

You feel that once you procure enough for future, you will begin partaking in your life. This is never going to occur. Go to any rich man and inquire as to whether he is happy with current monetary state? He needs increasingly more cash.

What you or your folks procuring today, was your fantasy pay immediately. Is it accurate to say that you are happy with that today? Regularly we work more on cash than bliss/wellbeing and so on and afterward utilize that cash to reestablish our wellbeing later on. Where is life then, at that point?

Dealing with the current first:

Allow us to zero in on the present. Do you put forth a similar attempt to appreciate today as much as to get your future. Today, you are more youthful than tomorrow. What you can appreciate today, you may not tomorrow. As Jim Rohn said, "Joy isn't something you delay for the future; it is something you plan for the present."

Do you deal with your wellbeing, family and qualities today? Today we show our youngsters how to bring in cash. Nonetheless, we don't help how to oversee things and live joyfully.

We are gathering/setting aside cash for future to have specialist/ clinical for our sicknesses. In any case, how we are doing keep up with our wellbeing today. Do you keep away from a lot of food on parties? Do you practice consistently for body? Would you contemplate for the tranquility of care? For what reason don't we essentially deal with ourselves at the primary spot?

There is nothing incorrectly in bringing in cash except for let us not cause our joy to rely upon it. That way you will continue to pause. Joy isn't about the amount you have yet how you appreciate with what you have. Regardless of how much cash you gather for your kids, in the event that you have not trained them to oversee it, it will all get lost.

Try not to think twice about own joy for your youngsters or future. On the off chance that you truly need to work on something for your children, cause them to figure out how to manage life challenges. Don't over secure them. Simply give them an establishment, set them free and let them sparkle.

Don't simply make your living here. God has sent every one of us on the earth to carry on with our life well. Partake in each second. Figure, how you might want to live today, so that there would be no lament tomorrow.

CHAPTER FOURTEEN

Why Procrastination Wins Over Creativity

Throughout everyday life, at some time you feel like you have something extraordinary in you. Something inventive that has a place just with you. It very well might be some sort of composing, singing, playing or even exercises like taking care of individuals around you. You want to show improvement over numerous others. You imagine that you can go on in your profession with it. Or on the other hand you believe you can show improvement over your every day work. You feel it as a your fantasy to accomplish. You choose to check it out full time or low maintenance.

In any case, over the long haul you stuck in your day by day life things. Then, at that point it's your psyche mind that starts giving a pardon to your inventiveness. You begin dreading consider the possibility that you don't think enough about it. Might be there are a lot more individuals with similar abilities all throughout the planet. You feel like previously crushed and you just let it go. And afterward after here and there the imaginative brain again wrecks on your head and same goes over and over.

Why it generally happens that your tarrying prevails upon your imagination. The appropriate response is straightforward. The fire needs oxygen to continue to consume. Here, the principal source as an oxygen is beginning Motivation. Alright, you got that as of now. Also, the second is Action. Also, between these two falsehoods delaying.

It is the hole between the primary activity and second activity that makes delaying wins. Never under any circumstance let delaying stops you get the second wellspring of oxygen. Make one stride. Take a little one and simply continue to take. Try not to fear disappointment. Try not to dread of awful results. Regardless of how awful you begins it will function as an establishment for the subsequent stage. Continue onward. Continue to commit errors, however not a similar one. Continue to gain from botches and get where you need to be.

Everybody has something imaginative inside, however achievement has a place with the individuals who recognize it and makes a move while fire is consuming.

Procrastination fuel of creativity :

Assuming the historical backdrop of innovativeness shows us anything, it is that extraordinary thoughts frequently come when we're least anticipating them. Consider Wolfgang Amadeus Mozart, who portrayed how new songs would show up while he was eating in a café, strolling after a supper or preparing for rest around evening time. "Those that please me, I hold, and even murmur; at any rate, so others have told me," he composed. "It appears to me difficult to say when they come to me and how they show up; what is sure is that I can't make them come when I wish."

Not simply Mozart encountered this peculiarity; the French mathematician Poincare depicted how his forward leaps happened while going on the transport or strolling by the ocean side, while Agatha Christie detailed that thoughts for her wrongdoing stories frequently came while cleaning up or having a shower. "I don't think need is the mother of development," she wrote in her collection of memoirs. "Creation, as I would see it, emerges straightforwardly from inaction, perhaps at the same time from apathy."

Clinicians would appear to concur, areas of strength for with that imaginative bits of knowledge are substantially more liable to happen after a time of "hatching" - in which you center around something completely not quite the same as the current task, while your mind works away in the background. This could incorporate going for a stroll, doing family tasks or having a shower. Indeed, even our stalling at work - like watching entertaining YouTube recordings - might be useful for our critical thinking, if it is done with some restraint.

CHAPTER FIFTEEN

Inspiration is Sufficiently Not, Right Motivation is What You Need

The huge distinction between individuals who have dreams and one who are really dealing with them is, Motivation.

A few group like you, keep themselves inspired each day. They learn about their fantasies, plan and make a few moves towards them. Inspiration is significant factor to get rolling. Be that as it may, in some cases inspiration doesn't function true to form. You invested parcel of energy perusing on the web or books, yet it doesn't have a lot of effect. Your life appear to be at a similar spot as it was yesterday and afterward you surrender after some time feeling that it can't be changed.

It very well may be valid for anything, for instance, assuming you need more satisfaction throughout everyday life or need a solid relationship or need to accomplish some monetary dream.

Do you see yourself today at a similar spot where you were yesterday, why?

Since

For instance, in case I am searching for the bliss, how much assist I with canning "Time Power" by Brian Tracy. Also, in case I am making progress toward Time the board, how accommodating "The Monk Who Sold His Ferrari" will be.

Allow me to reveal to you my own story in regards to perceiving the right inspiration.

I have been partial to self improvement and persuasive books. I have perused a lot of books in regards to satisfaction, usefulness, using time productively, achievement and different regions. Most likely, I am truly profited with every one of them. Yet, it doesn't occurred with the absolute first book.

At first, when I began perusing books I was simply searching for any persuasive book (from hit writers) in any book shop. I was so eager to take care of for my inspiration that, I couldn't have cared less about the sort of inspiration I was perusing. At some point it was minimal useful, yet more often than not It was not having a much effect (in the space I need), and here and there it was requiring some investment to complete that.

After at some point, I understood books that are having the genuine effect are those identified with region where I need to accomplish something. Then, at that point, I began zeroing in on explicit subject. Assuming I need more bliss, I took a gander at books regarding that matter. Indeed, it helped me understanding quick and polishes it off.

Distinguish your right inspiration:

Be explicit about the sort of inspiration you are searching for.

In case you are searching for more bliss, search out for Happiness books. In the event that you are searching for inventive plan to begin your business, chase for the innovativeness books and in case you are searching for better wellbeing ask books identified with them.

Something else I learned around then was:

"Never judge a book by its cover"

At the point when you begin perusing some book, you are giving your time (entirely of your life) to that. So pick carefully. Don't simply pass by its title. Peruse the synopsis in the back cover at any rate, it will give you much thought, what writer needs to say in that book? On the off chance that it sounds great to you, go get it.

Read constantly:

In case you can't track down the right book for you, simply don't quit perusing, rather start test.

Attempt books with various classifications. There are sufficient. What's more, you will begin understanding the right book for you when begin exploring different avenues regarding them. The book you will discover really intriguing and you simply don't ready to put it on table are book for you. In the event that you not ready to complete book you have picked since long time, the time has come to have a go at something new. Never stand by long an ideal opportunity to complete a book, pick another.

CHAPTER SIXTEEN

DREAMS IN LIFE

Why dreams are significant throughout everyday life?

Dreams rouse us to be what we need to be. All of us is one of a kind here. We as a whole need to soar. Who need to consider his to be as a normal? All things considered, there is no utilization of carrying on with a daily existence that doesn't go anyplace.

We as a whole dream. A few of us follow them with excitement and accomplish their fantasies. Some continue to stand by things to happen themselves and some just don't have the foggiest idea about the following stage. Allow us first to discuss initial step, Dreams.

Are your fantasies sensible?

What would you like to be throughout everyday life? On the off chance that you simply say I need to be fruitful, this isn't the practical answer. Achievement is an outcome not a fantasy. Be practical. How you measure your prosperity? Would you like to be fruitful creator, artist, entertainer, artist, specialist or business visionary? Exactness is significant.

Presently some says I need to be content throughout everyday life. What's more, let me advise you that "Bliss is venture not an objective". There will be joy as far as possible while you are following your fantasy energetically.

How to follow your fantasy?

Do you believe that wanting for something is barely enough to accomplish it? No. Of Course I trust in "The law of fascination" however we ought to be prepared to follow through on the cost to accomplish our fantasies too. You should think about your fantasies well overall and afterward follow the means. Study everything identified with your fantasies. Become acquainted with somebody who previously accomplished such sort of dreams. Utilize your time well. Each and every moment that is accessible, work on it.

How to draw nearer to your fantasies?

Dream ought to be sufficiently large to motivate you for your entire life and adequately little to boldness you to go on. Now and then our fantasy appears to be huge to such an extent that we stuck in the initial step. Do you wound up at a similar spot where you were last year? Break your fantasy into the objectives. So partition them into the means that you realize you can accomplish them inside certain time. Else they are only a wish and you can't go on.

Why dreams pass on?

Today the majority of us living another person's fantasy. They are doing a task that their folks need. Or then again they are working since they are procuring admirably to cover their bills. Some are doing privately-run company since they need to assume liability for it. However, as life passes a suspected comes into their psyche that is it worth living thusly.

At the point when individuals contemplate the fantasies they have in past, they feel lament since they are not taking care of business. They are watching their fantasies kicking the bucket.

Dreams and you

Envision yourself when you are lying in a medical clinic bed after a long time and pondering your life. Around then, do you envision lamenting the things that you ought to do now? Then, at that point do it now. Carry on with your fantasy life now. Try not to take help of reasons about family obligation or anything. You don't need to put all that to the side to begin chipping away at your fantasies. You can begin from nearly nothing. You can begin from half hour consistently. What's more, when things will continue you know answer of the entirety of your

CHAPTER SEVENTEEN

BE THE DRIVER OF YOUR LIFE BUS

Life is passing second by second. What's more, we won't ever know when we will be near an incredible finish.

How old you are? Have you carried on with your life the manner in which you need? Or then again would you say you are arranging this for what's to come?

Sadly there is no assurance for what's to come. What we have in our grasp is today. We are altogether riding in a transport called Life Bus getting into some heading. In the event that you realize that it won't the bearing you need, you need to alter today course since tomorrow it will past the point of no return.

The majority of us spend their today to make the present living. While some penance their today to get their future. A couple of us work for future as well as carry on with their life today too.

We as a whole carrying on with the existence venture, yet regularly we don't understand who is driving our Life Bus. We just let others drive our life transport. Figure, it very well may be your chief, your family or companions. We reclaim situate and become survivor of life venture. We go where things around us make us go.

We figure we don't have ability to change the things. This isn't the way. Get up and Take the driver seat. On the off chance that your life transport won't your objective, shift the course. Don't simply be survivor of your life, be the driver. Be the maker. Make your own life and make your own predetermination.

You are here on the earth to accomplish something extraordinary. Ask, your heart knows very well what it is. You have all the potential. You should carry on with an exceptional life. There could be no other amazing living being as human. So the thing would you say you are sitting tight for? Each second passing won't ever returned again.

There were innumerable individuals like you who figure they will change the world in future yet it won't ever come. Just not many of them understood the worth of today.

Are you expecting for better conditions following 5 or long term. Wonderful opportunity won't ever show up. Peruse the life story of any incredible individual from the set of experiences. It was never ideal everything for them when they began. However, when they began things began occurring. They didn't acknowledge what they don't need from life. They strived for what they need and in the long run got it by chipping away at it consistently. They were the driver of their life transport.

Try not to stand by so long. At that point, your life transport might have gone far away and might be you need to return a significant distance to begin your life venture once more. What's more, you won't ever have a lot of time then, at that point.

What you need from your life. How you need to be recollected. Why you need to matter in this world. Wake up and work for it.

CHAPTER EIGHTEEN

SELF CONTROL IS THE WAY TO SUCCESS;

You should all have heard the English saying "Where there is will, there is way". This is so obvious.

All of us needs to satisfy their fantasies throughout everyday life. However, a large portion of us feel that we need to do something exceptional to accomplish them. Then, at that point it comes to rationalize. Some says I need more time at the present time. Some says I need more abilities yet. In these reasons, they even disregard minimal that they can do at present time.

For instance, one of my companion need to assembled a web based shopping basket. Yet, he says it needs an excess of venture toward the start. It needs assets to purchase contracts from item proprietor just as to keep up with site and engineers. So he even had not ventured out.

Allow me to disclose to you that the initial step isn't to put away cash. The initial step is to consider what you really need. You ought to have the cycle and plans archived. Then, at that point you consequently track down your following stage and it won't be enormous to such an extent that you can't do it. You can generally begin from nearly nothing. Achievement sets aside time yet you ought to be resolved resolution en route.

Absence of Willpower:

Individuals don't begin something since they need will. Strength comes later. Do you recall whenever of your life when you were resolved to accomplish something and you did it? It very well may be some extreme test that you have passed or it very well may be some long outing that you at last have arranged.

On the off chance that we take a gander at our past we have number of things that we pleased with. The majority of these things were difficult, yet you got them in light of your will. You needed to do them at any expense. At the point when you have such self control, you will consistently figure out how to do this.

Try not to see five reasons why it ought not work, have faith in the one motivation behind why it should work.

Determination in every day life:

You don't should be at the moon to check your determination. It shows in your day to day existence consistently. Today this world is loaded with data. Regardless your calling is you will discover something new to learn. However, we need more an ideal opportunity to learn everything so we skip. Presently what matter is the significance of that thing and your self discipline to learn.

Assume you need to travel some slope station. You have charge/ Visa, yet you don't have the foggiest idea how to make online installment for advance enrollment. No doubt! We as a whole realize it is simple, however not for the person who is doing it interestingly. Presently in the event that you realize that you scarcely need to travel again and make online installment. You will discover simple way and request that some companion do it. You will send money to him later and it is finished. Okay.

Presently in the event that you realize that you regularly travel or you frequently need to make online installment. You need to discover that. For that you need to go to your companion and work on it. So you need some additional time and exertion right? Presently it goes to your determination. In the event that your will is solid you will figure out how to be with your companion and learn it. Yet, in the event that you need, will you will discover pardon. You will think that its simple to request that your companion's assist with doing it. Anyway it will tackle your motivation for brief time frame yet it will build your reliance over the long haul.

Illustration of Willpower:

I have consistently seen that when you keep away from something since you are not happy with it, it becomes beast. It takes solid resolution to defeat that dread.

This entire article motivated by one of my companion who came to me this Sunday. He needs to purchase something on the web yet he has never utilized his charge cards for exchange. He generally favored money buying or requested that a few companions stay away from the issue. In any case, this time he was resolved to make it by his own. As we as a whole realize that when we attempt to escape our adjust zone, things are troublesome particularly toward the start. It was Sunday morning and it was pouring modestly. So the simple choice was to keep away from this time once more. In any case, he didn't.

According to his words "I sit for some time and think that today it is coming down. Next Sunday, It might be excessively hot/cold. Close to Next Sunday I could have some pressing piece of work. After that it may be the case that my companion isn't accessible. So let go off these reasons and do it today. It might require some investment to discover a vehicle yet it isn't unimaginable. I could be minimal wet however so what."

So he escapes his home and came to me. It was difficult even after that. He bombed 6-7 times. Now and again due to program issue and once in a while it was requiring some investment to reset the secret phrase. Be that as it may, he didn't utilize my card to make installment and he at long last succeeded. It was all a result of his self discipline.

This was a basic model from day by day life. Yet, these basic assignments in day by day life test our resolution. On the off chance that we stall on these seemingly insignificant details, how might we accomplish enormous?

CHAPTER NINETEEN

Disappointment Means You Are in Race, Keep Going

In the event that you have large dreams, the expense would be enormous as well. Achievement comes at its cost. However, the vast majority of us quit attempting things, when meet with disappointment. When we fizzled, we figure we don't merit it or we don't have the ability to accomplish it. Yet, actually, one is consistently fit for accomplish anything he need enthusiastically. You simply need to continue onward.

"I have missed in excess of 9000 shots in my vocation. I have lost right around 300 games. On 26 events I have been endowed to make the match dominating effort... and missed. Furthermore, I have flopped again and again and over again in my life. Also, that is the reason I succeed" ~ Michael Jordan

We ought to comprehend that disappointment really assist us with developing, in the event that we gain from it. Do you think a life is worth in case there is no battle. You realize what occurs in the event that we get all we need, we don't esteem it. We comprehend benefit of something when we work for it or when we lost it (Its actual).

3 Things that help you continue to follow disappointment:

1.In the event that things turn out badly, don't miss the exercise: When something (or everything) is turning out badly in your way, don't miss the exercise. Since we as a whole do botches however significant is to quit messing up the same way over and over. Record the things you will take care when attempt sometime later.

2.Check where you slip, not where you fall: Whenever we start at something, a legitimate arranging is required. Now and then we are roused to the point that we take choices dependent on our feelings. By then we couldn't perceive imagine a scenario in which things won't function as wanted. So prior to beginning something important or contributing (cash just as time) in something, make bit by bit designs. You ought to know about every one of the snags that might come. Also, all things considered you ought to have elective ways to deal with continue onward.

3.Try not to think about disappointment literally: You are not your fantasy; your fantasy is only a piece of your life. So at whatever point you fall flat, don't take it sincerely for long time and search for the other options.

"At the point when one entryway shuts, another opens; however we regularly look so long thus remorsefully upon the shut entryway that we don't see the one which has opened for us." ~ Alexander Graham Bell

In the event that you fizzled at something, it implies you basically attempted and you are in front of thousand other people who don't attempt. Try not to join their club, on the off chance that you just bombed this time. Disappointment essentially implies you are in race. What's more, to dominate the race, as a matter of first importance you ought to be in the race. So dont surrender and attempt once again. You will get it. The very best.

CHAPTER TWENTY

Life Lessons from a Young kid in the Bus

I have seen a significant number of school graduates attempt to land position in their individual industry. In any case, subsequent to attempting 3 to a half year in the event that they don't get past, they surrender. They tell everybody that there are insufficient positions at this moment. Maybe I will say that there isn't sufficient energy in them at the present time.

Some of the time, an outsider can give us a remarkable life exercise. I might want to share an account of an energetic Young kid who met me on the transport.

Here, the story unfurls:

Recently, I was sitting tight for the transport to my office in Delhi. A little fellow came to me with a location and asked which transport will go to his ideal spot. I took a gander at him. He is by all accounts poor and new to the city. His objective was close to my office. Accordingly, I informed him concerning the right transport and we both took situates close to one another.

As it would have been venture around 45 minutes, we both began discussion to think about one another. In the first place, he got some information about my work. I disclosed to him that I am a Software Engineer. He has not been much mindful of the title "Programmer" yet he realizes that I work in the PC business. He appears to be too inquisitive and asked me that what I precisely do on PCs. I can see that he was inexperienced with the specialized terms of the IT/Computers yet I attempted to cause him to comprehend as additional as could be expected.

Presently it was my chance to ask what he makes his living. He revealed to me that he is looking for the work. He is from a little town and came in Delhi only fourteen days back. His schooling was slightly below average. He has quite recently done halfway (beneath graduation).

What that little youngster needed to do?

I got some information about what sort of occupation he needs to do. It was flabbergasted to hear that the needs to tackle work in PCs. He don't realizes how to work yet at the same time need to seek after in a PC work. He got some information about the choices he needs to work in this field. I advised him momentarily in as a simple language as could really be expected.

I came to realize that he was not searching for simply any work in PCs. For instance, I disclosed to him he could find out about PC equipment parts and quest for a PC fixing position. He denied it and said that he need to gain proficiency with the utilization of program and how to work them.

On the off chance that your eagerness is incredible, your troubles can't be extraordinary:

I told the little fellow that this isn't not difficult to find a new line of work he needs, as he doesn't have great instructive foundation.

He said, "I realize this isn't simple, however I have concluded that this is the thing that I need. A couple of months back, I used to terrified of the PC since I imagined that without English I was unable to learn PC. My English isn't acceptable. Presently I am here in the Capital of India, a long way from my little town. I'm here on the grounds that I need to battle my apprehensions. I need to set a model for individuals of my town. They are loaded with dread about the innovation. However, If I can do it, they can do it as well."

He proceeded, "Whatever it will take, I will do. I will begin from little yet won't sit inactive. I'm looking through different establishments around the city that offer different momentary seminars on various PC subjects/instruments. I'm simply analyzing the right measurement."

I accept that soon he will get what he needs.

Life Lessons gained from Young kid:

You can accept it as a basic tale about a hopeful little youngster or gain proficiency with an exercise about the life.

Have you chosen what you need to do throughout everyday life?

Choose what you need to do. Try not to do anything since everybody is doing it. Don't simply pursue cash. Get a new linc of work that fulfills you. It will assist you with long haul as opposed to transient fulfillment.

Do you have such commitment and enthusiasm to accomplish your fantasy?

How you feel about your fantasy? Do they fill you with enthusiasm? On the off chance that indeed, don't allow your dread to stop you. If not, Discover your actual dreams and begin following.

Today, the majority of individuals absence of confidence. They have a place with metro urban areas and they have well-rounded schooling. Since they didn't succeed yet, they mark themselves as a disappointment.

Keep in mind: Failure is just when you surrender. Hold up. It might require some investment, yet continue onward. Never let your fantasies kick the bucket within you. Try not to take a gander at the time that you have squandered. You can do it, as you are as yet alive.

CHAPTER TWENTY-ONE

WHY THE LAW OF ATTRACTION DOESN'T WORK FOR YOU

The Law of Attraction is the conviction that "Like draws in Like". As per this law, "You are drawing in sure and negative things in life by zeroing in on certain or negative contemplations".

Napoleon Hill over and again referred to in his books about The Law of Attraction to make the progress.

There is a heavenly soul in every one of us. The spirit assumes a significant part in The Law of Attraction. As our body needs food to remain solid, our spirit needs musings. Every one of our contemplations supports our spirit. In this way, the force of our spirit simply relies on the nature of our musings.

The spirit has preeminent force that assists us with getting what we need. It additionally assists us with getting what we don't need also. This is the place where we call; The Law of Attraction doesn't work. In all actuality, The Law of Attraction consistently works, yet you don't know that it is working the other way.

The Law of Attraction couldn't care less "what you need" or "what you don't need". It basically reacts to your considerations.

"Individuals contemplate what they don't need and draw in business as usual"

At last, musings are the things. We generally think little of the force of the musings. Never question it. We are altogether similar to a magnet. Whatever we are thinking we are drawing in.

Would you like to make The Law of fascination works for you? Here is the thing that you need to do: Shift your concentration from "what you don't need" to "what you need".

I have gone to a Meet-up last week in New Delhi. We talked about, Why The Law of Attraction doesn't work for a few? Here is my decision:

6 reasons why The Law of Attraction doesn't work for you:

1.Core interest: You need to check where your center is. Once more, your emphasis ought to be on "what you need to have" instead of on "what you would prefer not to have." Visualize what you need to have and you will have it.

2.Conviction: Belief is the establishment. Put stock in yourself. Put stock in your musings and be explicit. You ought to have an unmistakable picture of what you want. For model, assuming you need to be a tycoon by winning a lottery you don't put stock in yourself. You have confidence in karma. As a matter of fact, you don't accept, you are simply wishing. Assuming you need to be a very rich person by seeking after in one of your calling, I can say that you trust in yourself.

3.Dread: I have consistently seen two sorts of dread when we begin something. In the first place, The Fear of Failure. Individuals dread imagine a scenario in which you would fall flat. It is preferably better to fall flat over not attempting by any stretch of the imagination. Second, The Fear of Success. Shockingly, a few group even dread on the off chance that they can deal with the achievement or not. Consequently, they discovered agreeable to be disappointment at the main point. The lone thing you need to fear is simply the dread. Win it.

4.Uncertainty: People question in the event that they can possibly accomplish their fantasies and fabricate limits to them. The law of Attraction manages job when brain is open. Try not to allow your uncertainty to stop you. Everybody can do what he truly needs to do. "The universe likes SPEED. Try not to delay, don't re-think, don't question."

5.Negative Thoughts: As I have effectively said that, the nature of contemplations decides how "The Law of Attraction" works for you. I have seen that more often than not, we partner negative contemplations with every one of our positive thoughts. One of my companions consistently needs to begin own business. He accepts that he can do it, however always unable to begin. Why The Law of Attraction doesn't work for him? I can see that he is extremely sure when he says, "I can do it". In any case, soon after these positive considerations he thinks for some time and a few reasons that why he may not ready to get achievement in that. Therefore, for each and every sure idea, he a few negative musings. What do you figure which musings will draw in additional? That is the reason the law of fascination doesn't work for the most.

6.Secret language: I accept that "The Law of the Attraction" is the mysterious language of the god. Not every person can hear it. To start with, you need to put stock in it. Then, at that point you need to hang tight for the ideal opportunity. Then, at that point you will get looks at it. It took me around four months, when I begin seeing that the law of nature is assisting me with accomplishing my fantasies. There will be small clues around your fantasy venture. You need to discover them. It might require some investment however "The Law of Attraction truly works".

CHAPTER TWENTY-TWO

TRY NOT TO REST, DO YOUR BEST : 1

Have you accomplished your best throughout everyday life? On the off chance that indeed, no compelling reason to peruse further. Rest and rest.

In the event that you have not carried on with your best life yet, don't rest. Rather than unwinding, give a valiant effort.

While carrying on with the life, we regularly become exceptionally sluggish. We simply accomplish our normal work, eat, rest and rest. The vast majority of our standard work is a task that you are doing only for your living. We never feel enough propelled to do anything extra for our life. We generally fail to remember that we have a few dreams to chip away at.

Ask any specialist. What do you do after your customary work?

Ask any lady in the house. What do you do after your day by day home errands?

Ask any understudy. What do you do at home after your school schoolwork?

Request all from them, what do you do toward the end of the week or get-aways. The greater part of them will say, "I do partake in a piece and take rest". Satisfaction is incredible. As Bertrand Russell cited, "The time you appreciate burning through isn't sat around idly". All things considered, what is the utilization of living in the event that we hate.

I will discuss the other thing called "rest" or "unwinding". Why we need rest? The amount we need to unwind. Allow us to see.

Why we need rest?

By the day's end, every one of us needs to unwind. However, what amount? It is a great idea to have a brief break between the work to feel invigorated and empowered. It is good to unwind for half or an hour subsequent to doing your day task. It is totally fine to partake in a film or an excursion toward the end of the week. Yet, how would you manage the remainder of your time. Definitely I know. You spent it staring at the TV the entire day. You wrap up and unwind.

Today you are burning through your time very much like that. You think you merit that. You are expecting that tomorrow will carry you more opportunity to chip away at your fantasy projects. Allow me to remind you my companion, you will have more duties with the time too.

Do you rest for your body?

In more seasoned days, the majority of our every day work included proactive tasks. Today, there are machines surrounding us. Our actual exertion so much decreased via programmed innovation. Accordingly, I accept that our body never needs that amount rest. Shockingly, the majority of us went through an entire day of end of the week for rest. We become dependent on rest since we over and again do that. Change it; it is about the propensity.

CHAPTER TWENTY-THREE

Try not to Rest, Do your Best : 2

Would you rest for your care?

Offer rest to your psyche. Today, the vast majority of our work includes mind power as opposed to our actual force. So unwind for some time, yet again don't try too hard. Set a restricted opportunity to unwind. You know well overall, in the event that you set your psyche free for quite a while, it brings numerous musings. The majority of these considerations are about the past or future, which brings strain and uneasiness.

You realize numerous individuals rest the entire day and still feel tired. Accomplish something you love and you never feel tired. Hold onto the day.

Is it accurate to say that you are shy of time?

We generally rationalize that we don't have a lot of time to accomplish something remarkable throughout everyday life. Allow me to ask you a certain something. What do you do when got brief period after your work? We as a whole got little bits of time each day. A large portion of us squander it never helping to call it "Rest".

What will "rest" bring you toward the finish of life?

Assume. Today, you don't have anything to do. In this manner, you are wrapping up. You will feel better while resting. However, In the finish of your life, do you recall any of your resting day. No. You will recollect just days in which you have accomplished something.

You will recall the days that transformed you. You will recollect the days when you completely changed someone.

Make your days noteworthy by accomplishing something amazing each day. What? Would you be able to do extraordinary things consistently? Alright. In any event, don't sit inactive. Make one minuscule stride each day. Do the easily overlooked details in an incredible manner. This will make the extraordinary contrasts with the time.

The most effective method to begin putting forth a valiant effort:

Assuming you need to change your propensity, you need to change your reasoning first. You think you aren't anything in this world and that is the reason, "Nothing on the planet is more normal than fruitless individuals with ability."

Master Vivekananda says, "How might we be nothings. We are everything, prepared to do everything. We can do everything, and Men should do everything."

It is our convictions that restrict us. Take a gander at the historical backdrop of the incredible individuals. They have not given exceptional forces. They didn't have 48 hours per day. They didn't have two minds. Neither had they had four hands. All things considered, they did their best since they didn't rest. It was the confidence of our progenitors that make them go and made them extraordinary.

So next time when somebody asks you, "What do you do at the end of the week?" Never say, "I simply wrap up." Instead, say, "I give a valiant effort."

Be energetic about putting forth a valiant effort throughout everyday life. Rather than loosening up entire time, work on yourself. Work on something for the others. Leave a more wonderful world. Try not to stop until you accomplish all that you genuinely need throughout everyday life.

CHAPTER TWENTY-FOUR

Interior Rewards and External Rewards

What moves you to follow your fantasies? All that we do throughout everyday life, we accomplish for remunerations. Award is anything given in acknowledgment of administration, exertion, or accomplishment. There are two sorts of remunerations: Internal Rewards and External Rewards.

Outside Rewards:

An outside or extraneous prize comes from outer source. It very well might be some prize, decoration, prize, testament, or cash.

Inner Rewards:

An inner or characteristic award is the thing that you experience inside. It is pride from with-in. It is encountering the fulfillment comes from your own behavior.

What is the greatest inspiration in your life: Internal Rewards or External Rewards? Tragically, the vast majority of us pursue outside remunerations.

How External prizes drives our life:

Today assuming we need to seek after our fantasy, interest, or calling, we first check it on the boundary of outside remunerations. Would i be able to procure more in some other calling? Are there enough freedoms to get acknowledgment in this? Will I have a protected future and stipend in this field?

Assume you are procuring admirably as a designer. In the interim you found that you can cook well and you appreciate cooking more than your designing. Presently you might have an option for your calling. Notwithstanding, prior to seeking after, you first search for same outside remuneration as you are getting in designing.

As you are now in a very much settled calling, you won't attempt to emerge from your agreeable zone. This is the way pressing factor of outer prizes restricts our life. Regardless of how great we are in singing, composing, or playing, we don't think them as a calling.

Significance of Internal Rewards:

The majority of us need to be effective by bringing in cash and popularity. Now and again we accomplish nearly everything in life yet at the same time find that something is absent. This happens when our life is loaded with outside remuneration yet absence of inside remuneration.

In the event that your calling inspired basically by outer motivation, you will battle for deep rooted fulfillment. Whatever you do throughout everyday life, first do it for yourself. You realize what fulfills you. You realize what is near your heart. Continuously rely on your instinct.

"In the event that you don't cherish what you are doing, you basically squandering your life."

Outside Rewards follows Internal Rewards:

In the start of any calling, our attention ought to be on Internal Rewards. We should zero in on learning, self-investigation and satisfaction. At the point when you follow your fantasies spurred by inside remunerations, outer prizes follow. You will get more than your opinion.

Joy is enormous Reward:

Life is an excursion. What is the pleasant arriving at an objective on the off chance that you hate venture by any means. Your fantasy or your objective or even your calling ought to be something that rouses you inside. Then, at that point life will be a great ride.

We as a whole have no less than one thing that we simply love accomplishing for ourselves. It very well might be playing a game. It very well might be singing. Might be you compose on the grounds that you love to do it. We do these things regardless of whether they don't present to us any outside remunerations.

CHAPTER TWENTY-FIVE

LIFE ISN'T FOR ALL INTENTS AND PURPOSES HOWEVER AS WE ARE

We as a whole have alternate point of view about existence. A few of us see positive parts of whatever occurs. While some continue to fault that life is a struggle. Why a few sees excellence of the nursery while some see, dry leaf and waste dissipated en route. Why a few of us change the conditions around them and some change themselves according to conditions.

All things considered, the external world is simply an impression of our inward world. How you feel is the way you see the world. We see life not all things considered but rather as we are.

In case you are steady inside, nothing in the external world can shake you. In case you are cheerful inside, occasions outside can not influence you. Be that as it may, if your joy relies just upon outer climate and individuals, you will battle for enduring joy.

Impact of Circumstances and Situations:

A few group play the round of their life according to their own guidelines while some basically react to the environmental factors. Keep in mind: No matter how hard the conditions are, you have the ability to abrogate them. Your conditions are feeble without your force.

Why we become a captive of conditions once in a while? We feel like casualty when things run wild. God gives you issue according to your ability you know. Next time when a test shows up throughout everyday life, think yourself more remarkable than the issue. As Charles F. Lummis said, "I'm greater than whatever can happen to me."

Troubles in life exist to make us solid. When you know this craft of life, you can manage any test. When you go through troubles, you become an alternate individual. Figure out how to gain from inconvenience and let it go.

Pick Thoughts carefully:

Everybody has diverse nature on the planet. What makes an individual person all things considered? Conditions? No. You probably seen individuals with various arrangement of perspectives in similar conditions. What makes one unique in relation to other is their perspective and the perspective make distinctive lifestyle.

It is safe to say that you are mindful of the force of musings? Considerations have a significant effect in the character. They can be dangerous and valuable. In light of these musings we respond or react to the circumstances throughout everyday life. Also, contingent upon the characteristics of musings our life turn up or down.

The uplifting news is, we can pick our musings thus the nature of our life. When you become mindful of the realities that you can assume responsibility for your psyche, you can handle your life. You can carry on with an existence of your motivation.

You can't generally control your brain powerfully. Condescend to it. As you manage a kid with adoration and empathy, would it with your care. Reflection can help in an incredible manner.

Your convictions forever:

Convictions framed throughout the time since we conceived. In the "Stir the goliath inside", Tony Robbins says once we structure a conviction, we channel every one of the data dependent on those convictions. We once in a while inquiries to our convictions. What we accept is more imperative to us than what we see.

On the off chance that you make them limit convictions, you will continue to belittle yourself. The no one but thing can break your example is to question your self-restricting convictions. Our convictions shape our life. Notwithstanding, in the event that you accept that you can't accomplish something, you would not ready to do it.

The vast majority of the choices we take unknowingly dependent on these convictions. Subsequently, in the event that you have solid convictions that you can accomplish something, you will make a positive move. On the off chance that you have question that you can't do, you will in general keep away from it by rationalizing.

Our convictions basically dependent on references and encounters of ourselves and different people. We can discover references to help or go against our convictions. It is fundamental for center around the references or encounters to help the conviction that you can do it.

Make a Life you need:

A significant number of us simply pass their life sitting tight for quite a long time and occasions. For what reason don't we hold onto consistently? For what reason don't we live each day?

Do you have a feeling of fulfillment and euphoria the entire day? Is it accurate to say that you are carrying on with a day to day existence you need? If not, the time has come to assume responsibility for your life.

You are brought into the world to carry on with life your way. Your musings make your life. It is an ideal opportunity to support your musings. The time has come to beat the convictions that are restricting you. Try not to stand by any longer. Make a stride ahead. Do it now. You dream life is holding up you

CHAPTER TWENTY-SIX

KEEP YOURSELF MOTIVATED

We as a whole know the force of inspiration. At the point when we are spurred, we experience such an incredible self that no fantasy is too huge for us.

Do you recall when you heard a rousing story and right away felt loaded with inspiration? Around then, you should want to accomplish something exceptional throughout everyday life. Be that as it may, the following day all inspiration evaporates away.

At the point when we pay attention to an inspirational tune or watch any persuasive film, we feel on the highest point of the world. They remind us our fantasies. We feel so empowered. Nonetheless, the inspiration keep going for some time. Then, at that point, we make ourselves battle with the troubles of day by day life. We start to lose confidence in ourselves. At last, we disregard our fantasies.

Inspiration: The Secret of Success:

Do you realize what makes incredible individual extraordinary? Which isolates them from others? How effective individuals can accomplish objectives in a steady progression? The principal mysterious of their prosperity is Motivation. Effective individuals live in inspiration. Indeed, they are brimming with inspiration constantly.

It's not possible for anyone to remain inspired until the individual in question consistently effectively re-energizes himself with inspiration. Fruitful individuals have a lot of persuasive sources to a great extent. At whatever point they figure out some time, they feed themselves with inspiration. Do you do it?

The most effective method to Keep Yourself Motivated:

At whatever point I talk about having enduring inspiration, a pleasant piece of the Zig Ziglar quote comes into my psyche.

Today we frequently rationalize that we need more time every day. Allow me to disclose to you that you don't have to save 30 minutes consistently only for inspiration. Accordingly, there is no compelling reason to rationalize. You just need to take little bits of time every day to keep yourself roused.

Tune in or read something motivational only two or three minutes and you will feel inspired for a few hours. It is dependent upon you, when you can figure out that watches. For instance, you can take care of inspiration yourself each day. You can even do it while shaving or scrubbing down. You can do it while driving or voyaging. So, propel yourself at whatever point you figure out time.

Instructions to ride on the Motivation:

Inspiration resembles a fuel for the vehicle. It assists you with beginning life vehicle for your fantasy venture. Presently, on the off chance that you keep your life vehicle at a similar spot regardless of whether it has begun, all your fuel will lose all sense of direction to no end. So utilize your persuasive fuel before it closes. How?

When you feel inspired, make moves toward dreams. Thus, these activities will keep you inspired for long time.

A considerable lot of us have an enormous hole between the reasoning and activities. Thinking alone never makes a difference. There are uncounted quantities of individuals who think a ton. Numerous individuals dream and prepare to stun the world. Nonetheless, instead of making the following stride, they sit tight for supernatural occurrences. They trust that the more inspiration will come. They hang tight for the chances.

Meet the Motivation frequently:

In the event that inspiration doesn't come to it, you let it all out. In the event that a chance doesn't come, make it. You never understand your actual force. The entirety of the extraordinary individuals of their time resembled us. The vast majority of them were not conceived skilled. They found their thought process. They fostered their ability. They roused themselves and accomplished their fantasies. That is it.

CHAPTER TWENTY-SEVEN

VENTURE OUT TOWARD YOUR DREAM

At the point when we understand our fantasies, life gets some information about it. Then, at that point, it is fundamental for venture out toward your fantasy venture. Be that as it may, the hardest piece of excursion is this initial step.

What is the initial step for you? Allow me to clear a certain something. The initial step isn't simply contemplating your fantasy. Here, initial step implies one activity step that set out an establishment for your fantasy. The majority of the disappointments in this world happen not long before this initial step.

Take a model. Assuming you need to be an author, simply contemplating it won't make you one. Venture out and Start composing. On the off chance that you can't, learn it first. Join a class. Go to an occasion or Read a book. Don't simply sit inactive. You can begin little.

You can become anything in the event that you begin chipping away at it. The solitary restriction you have to you. On the off chance that you don't venture forward, you will remain at a similar spot. As Liz Smith said, "Start some place; you can't assemble a standing on what you mean to do."

Why Begin?

At the point when our fantasies are new, we are amped up for them. Indeed, even contemplating it can feel you with enthusiasm. Around then, we assemble numerous plans in our psyche. As time pass by, inspiration factor gets reducing. Why? Since, we keep think a great deal and don't go past reasoning.

First and foremost, many dread variables stop us to settle on early choices. Now and then our uncertainty and now and then there is dread of disappointment forestall us to start. Keep in mind:

What are the angles that stop us venturing out? Allow us to perceive and begin dealing with them today.

Why venture out toward Your Dreams:

1.You will escape your Comfortable Zone: You can't start since it might take you to the awkward zone. Keep in mind, the most noteworthy development lie when you escape your agreeable zone. Get out and Fly high.

2.You will learn along the Journey: You might fear beginning something since you don't think a lot about the necessary abilities. It is okay. No one is amazing here as flawlessness is a deep rooted measure. You might learn quicker once the perfect excursion start.

3.You make one stride, God will take two: If you move toward your objective, God will find two ways to help you. Notwithstanding, you must be persistence first and foremost and continue onward.

4.You Vision will turn out to be clear: Do you have question in your latent capacity? When you will make a move, every one of your questions disappear. You will actually want to see your objective plainly. In the event that your activities are not propelling you, it isn't for yours. In the event that you actually question yourself, stop it. In the event that you loath what you are doing, accomplish something that energetic you.

5.You will lose your Fear of Failure: When you begin something, not all things go true to form. Disappointments occur throughout everyday life. It is OK to bomb however never rehash a similar error. Disappointments consistently offer us greatest exercises of life. Might be without that disappointment you would never investigate a few measurements. As Japanese axiom, "Fall multiple times, stand up eight."

6.You will see Unlimited Opportunities: Sometimes we surrender our fantasies since we don't see a lot of chance. In the start of anything, we can't actually assess the degree. Today, the world is brimming with promising circumstances that were never exists prior. You will see a lot of ways continuing to your fantasy when you venture out.

CHAPTER TWENTY-EIGHT

YOUR DETERMINATION DETERMINES YOUR DESTINY

What is your fantasy life? What sort of predetermination you need to make for yourself? At a certain point, we understand what it very well may be. In any case, it continues to change with the time. We will in general have another fantasy or objectives on the grounds that the previous one appears to be difficult to accomplish.

Why we continue to change objectives in our Life?

We choose something. We work on it energetically. Then, at that point we experience difficulties and our enthusiasm begins decreasing. Before long we think we are not sufficiently fit and we quit. We take up another objective and the equivalent follows.

As a matter of fact, when we take any choice, we are extremely certain about its prosperity however nature consistently has plans to test our assurance.

Is it accurate to say that you are the one in particular who thinks beyond practical boundaries?

Do you imagine that you are one of rare sorts of people who think beyond practical boundaries? No. A large portion of the world hopes against hope to become tycoon. There are numerous who need to become well known on the planet. Numerous thinks beyond practical boundaries in their day to day existence. Notwithstanding, a large portion of them fall flat. Why? All things considered, after a little exertion, it appears to be intense or inconceivable with the time.

Victors are standard individuals with uncommon assurance. We fizzle since we need assurance. On the off chance that we check, it isn't just that we come up short at enormous things. We bomb day by day at little things for a similar explanation: assurance.

Here are a portion of the normal assertions of our every day life:

1.I will get up ahead of schedule from tomorrow onwards.

2.I will begin morning walk or reflection one week from now.

3.I will begin concentrate for my test or plan for a superior occupation from tomorrow.

4.I will stop smoking from today.

You more likely than not made comparable sort of guarantees with yourselves. What occur with them frequently? I realize we start (some of the time). In any case, it last just for few days and you came to realize that it isn't some tea. These easily overlooked details can tell that how resolved you are.

Do you anticipate that a straight journey should your fantasies?

You need to seek after your own business or on the other hand assuming you need to go into an organization, you imagined. You need to change your calling. You need to turn into a craftsman. These objectives lead you to fate you imagined for yourself.

How might you abandon battle? In the event that it very well may be easy to accomplish those fantasies, many would have been effective in this world. Notwithstanding, you realize that the extent of effective people isn't so high.

I have seen ordinarily that individuals accept circumstances for what they are. We continue going until everything is acceptable. At whatever point we discovered some opposition, our methodology/ eagerness began biting the dust. In this way, the greater part we had always wanted don't have life. Try not to allow that to happen to you.

Before you begin anything, understand that what challenges you might get. In case you are totally ready with the standards of the game, your odds to win will increment. We can't decide every one of the difficulties that we might get. Nonetheless, we might anticipate large numbers of them and get ready for them ahead of time so they don't come shockingly to obliterate your arrangements.

Guides to test your Determination:

Allow us to perceive how nature will test how resolved you are with straightforward models from day by day life:

Do you recall, when you chose to read and plan for your test or next work from tomorrow? In the long run, you will wind up occupied tomorrow more than some other day. It is possible that couple of visitors went to your home and your arranging is upset. Is it accurate to say that you were ready to proceed with what you chosen?

You chose to go for a stroll or start work out. In the wake of doing a few days, you stayed with some work in office. You arrived behind schedule at home and your body requests a more rest following day. Along these lines, you can't get up promptly toward the beginning of the day and your chose skip it for a day. Did you give that sort of reasons to skip what you have begun?

You chose to stop your annoyance/smoking and need to improve personally. Abruptly, you will confront circumstances more muddled than you typically need to achieve that. Will you gripe that the world doesn't need you to turn out to be better?

Why this occurs? Why circumstances appear to be more troublesome when we begin something? All things considered, that is when nature check whither your choice is transitory or perpetual. What to do straightaway?

Be resolved with your choices:

Assurance is about the strength of your psyche to get rolling in any event, when a circumstance doesn't favors you. The greater your fantasy or objectives is, the more you fall into difficulty. Each issue is a type of challenge and freedom to develop.

At whatever point you want to fall or when things are not occurring true to form, say to yourself, "This might take minimal longer, however it will occur."

Recollect that the more you can manage these difficulties, the greater will be rewards that life gives you.

Never let your state of mind obliterate your arrangements:

Frequently we become a captive of our mind-sets. Regardless of whether you have some time, you come up with rationalization that I don't have mind-set to contemplate. Regardless of whether your cautions reveal to you that it is an ideal opportunity to awaken as you chose yesterday. You say, "I'm not in disposition today. Might be I have better disposition tomorrow" and you switch off the alert.

Try not to rely upon you dispositions. On the off chance that you chose, get up and do what needs to be done. A choice resembles your guarantee to yourself. Keep the worth of your words. In the event that you don't, you are cheating with yourselves and your fantasies.

On the off chance that you come up with rationalization once, nature will give both of you more motivation to tarry. On the off chance that you make a stride, nature will think of two stages to help you.

Continue onward:

Reconsider seeking after any objective. Be that as it may, when you choose, give it an activity. Try not to stop from that point. Little activity is sufficient to keep you on target and persuade you to continue.

Difficulties will come to make you more grounded. Make a big difference for learning and keep and you will get it one day.

As Michael Jordon said, "Hindrances don't need to stop you. In the event that you run into a divider, don't pivot and surrender. Sort out some way to climb it, go through it, or work around it."

CHAPTER TWENTY-NINE

HOW TO DEAL WITH THE POSSIBILITY OF BEING AWESOME?

How to deal with the possibility of being awesome?

Search for flawlessness. That is fine. Attempt to get things done on par with conceivable. That is good. However, don't quit doing this is on the grounds that you can't do it consummately. Make a stride and continue to learn. You will improve while doing this.

"Take a stab at persistent improvement, rather than flawlessness." ~ Kim Collins

Flawlessness? It is at the forefront of everyone's thoughts. When I will switch my present place of employment, I will seek after my fantasy. When I will procure this much, I will begin my business. When I will have additional time, I will begin going to the rec center. When I will have less obligations, I will begin partaking in my life.

How flawlessness has annihilated your fantasy:

Here is an another model:

You need to turn into a craftsman like an artist, essayist, painter or anything. Assume, you got an opportunity to take part in an occasion and feature your capacity. In the event that you attempt to discover a pardon that you have not arranged well. That implies you are holding up flawlessness. Don't simply pass up on the chance.

Alright! Its done. It is okay in case it was not great. Continue To learn:

We went for a meeting, however it turned out poorly.

We are simply back from occasion trip, however couple of things left to investigate.

We are simply back from a film which we went with elevated standards, yet it turned out lesser than that (or calamity).

It is OK in case it was not great.

We frequently end up with frustration, since we or something failed to meet expectations our assumptions. Things don't generally occurs in our manner. Life is energizing, since it is flighty. The mystery of enduring joy is to partake in the excursion and learn constantly. As Eugene Delacroix said, "The craftsman who focuses on flawlessness in everything accomplishes it in nothing."

Subsequently, it is OK in the event that you don't sing awesome. It is OK, on the off chance that you don't play consummately. It is insightful to acknowledge that we can't dominate at everything. Continue to do it as long as you prefer it. Continue moving and Keep appreciating.

CHAPTER THIRTY

TRY NOT TO HANG TIGHT FOR PERFECTION, START NOW!

At the point when we have dreams, we have an energy. At the point when we have an enthusiasm, we need to do it with Perfection.

Regularly, when we have a few objectives, we need to begin it with an impact. We need to turn into an overnight star. We need to accomplish best at the earliest opportunity. Yet, things set aside time. It improves with the time, however the key is to begin as quickly as time permits.

What happens is that we have a thought, which we think can change our or somebody's life in a flash. In any case, we don't deal with it until we have positive circumstances. We hang tight for additional time and more assets. What's more, one day another person assembled an item on that thought and we lament.

We have heard this proclamation, "Ohh I likewise had a similar thought, yet couldn't begin."

How Perfection frequently turns out our greatest foe?

At first, when a thought goes into our brain, it takes a ton of time. We don't have adequate data at first. We have some uncertainty in your psyche and the most noticeably awful of everything is that you need to begin it great. No, that is unimaginable more often than not. This sensation of "I will do it great" regularly stops us before we start.

Think for some time, how long we squander prior to taking the primary action towards our objective. What happens is this. You were going to begin and afterward you understand that You can improve. You stop it between and say that I will do it tomorrow in a superior manner.

Scarcely any day passed and you lost interest in that thought. It very well may be your business thought or something about your fantasy.

CHAPTER THIRTY-ONE

TRACK DOWN YOUR TALENT

Distinguish your Talent:

As Buddha said, "Everybody is gifted here, however a few of us never opened their bundle". Have you opened your bundle?

Where would you be able to discover your ability? You can discover it in your interests. You might be brought into the world with some normal gift. You can discover your ability in your abilities gained during training. It very well might be through composition, talking, programming, planning, painting, singing, or overseeing representatives or client. It very well might be improving home or cooking. It very well may be anything.

Once in a while we just disregard our ability since it appears to be something normal to us. For a model as a homemaker, you get ready nourishment for your family. You realize that you cook well and you as it doing. Accordingly, you may be asking yourself, "How might it be an ability? This is my normal work and each homemaker like me is doing it."

There ought to be no doubt to ability as large, little or normal ability. An ability is an ability. In the event that anybody asks you, what your ability is? Let's assume it gladly that, "I can cook well". On the off chance that you like your ability, you provide it another guidance to advance. No one can really tell where it might take you in your life.

"With normal abilities and unprecedented constancy, everything is feasible." ~ Sir Thomas Fowell Buxton

On the off chance that you have completed your schooling and don't yet know your ability, you are getting past the point of no return. In case you are working together or tightening position and don't have the foggiest idea about your ability, you are tricking yourself. 33% of your life previously passed and you don't have the foggiest idea what you truly need to do in this world?

Try not to stand by excessively long. Pay attention to your gut and rely on your instinct. Recognize once and trust on it. You can generally sharp your ability by mastering required abilities later.

Utilize your ability:

It is Showtime presently; utilize your ability. When you distinguish your calling of heart, don't sit inactive. Try not to hold your ability sitting tight for the ideal time or more freedoms. As Ivan Panin said, "Not he merits acclaim that has gifts, but rather he that utilizes them."

Ability won't work, on the off chance that you don't. It won't motivate you on the off chance that you don't make any move about it. The delight isn't in dreaming about your ability, yet in utilizing that ability. Utilize your ability. Venture out and investigate the measurements.

CHAPTER THIRTY-TWO

EVERYBODY HAS TALENT YET NOT EVERYONE USE IT

In this world, individuals have a place with three classifications:

1.Who has ability – (Everyone has)

2.Who realizes they have ability. – (Some of us knows)

3.Who really utilize their ability – (Only a couple qualify here)

At the point when we are youthful and completing our schooling, we realizes what makes us alive. We have confidence in our fantasies. We know our specialities. Frequently we fail to remember our ability when we pick our calling dependent on our instructive capability and authentication. We disregard our advantage and specialization and our ability begin disappearing.

Have you at any point asked yourself, what is your ability? Do you question on the off chance that you have any? Which classification you fall into? Allow us to find.

Everybody has Talent:

Everybody is brought into the world with potential to do unprecedented throughout everyday life. Sadly, we settled customary. At the point when somebody asks what our ability is, we think for some time and say that we don't have any ability.

Much of the time, we have never attempted to investigate our ability. Everybody is remarkable in one manner or other. Regardless of whether you analyze an individual with inabilities, you will discover something unique inside him. Hence, Never ever, question your reality in this world.

Now and then we just fail to remember it. Do you recollect when you get some celebration stuff to adorn your home? You use it for a couple of days and afterward keep it in store to utilize it later. Numerous years some other time when you are cleaning your home, you in the end discover your stuff. Then, at that point you understand that you nearly fail to remember it.

On the off chance that you don't utilize things for some time, you absolutely disregard them. The equivalent occur with ability. Do you fail to remember something that was your forte once? Allow us to perceive how to discover the gift that nature given us.

For what reason is disclosure significant?

Apparently, nobody has been conceived who has a deep understanding of themselves. Simply focus on those great high school years, on the off chance that you want an update. So life is an excursion of disclosure. We find what our identity is, what we have confidence in, what we like and aversion. Also, assuming that we are strong in our excursion of revelation, we won't ever stop.

Envision where you would be personally in the event that you had at any point totally quit finding. In the event that you halted sufficiently early, you probably won't have the option to walk, read or compose. Others may very well never have figured out how to swim, ride a bicycle or drive a vehicle. Shouldn't something be said about writing and the creative mind, where might they be assuming you had quit finding? Not many individuals are at any point here, or possibly not really for all around while. To wait there would have all the earmarks of being an exceptionally sluggish passing of the soul.

Many individuals are in a condition of detached revelation, they don't effectively go out searching for new things, new encounters or new information, yet it appears every once in a while and visits them. Reports about medicines for infections, logical revelations or extraordinary achievements could be instances of this.

Network programs about extraordinary individuals, incredible experiences and odd creatures. In any event, understanding books, verifiable, fiction or even magazines; all can give fascinating pieces of disclosure. Do you have any idea what tatting is and the way that it connects with different types of texture workmanship? Truly, it was on TV.

Certain individuals are in a more dynamic condition of revelation, in some measure in certain parts of their lives. When did you last gain proficiency with another game (chess, go, checkers, Monopoly or Life)? Another expertise (welding, shuffling or carpentry)? Another dialect (or worked at expanding the dominance of a language you are now acquainted with)?

When was the last time you proceeded to take on an actual test that you had no genuine thought how to appropriately do (skydiving, SCUBA jumping or rock climbing)? Physical, mental, and profound are parts of revelation that can be sought after, would you say you are searching for another experience?

CHAPTER THIRTY-THREE

INSPIRATIONAL ARTICLES FOR STUDENTS TO GETTING SUCCESS : 1

Motivation isn't just to actuate an individual's craving for riches yet in addition to enact an individual's life energy and stir the inventive excitement of a country. These after persuasive articles for understudies aggregated by the proofreader for everybody.

Present day instructive brain science accepts that there are numerous motivators and intends to spur understudies to get achievement is all inclusive and successful. Achievement inspiration is the inspiration for understudies to effectively seek after accomplishments and desire to succeed. Clinicians accept that it should turn into the principle inspiration for understudies' homeroom learning. Here we have demonstrated that Student inspiration articles for progress and encountering the delight of achievement can extraordinarily work on their learning.

How Students Motivate Yourself to Study Hard:

Learning is a long lasting thing. As the idiom goes, it's great to learn as you live. Understudies need to learn. So how understudies inspire yourself to concentrate hard?

Think about your own life plan:

We will have numerous activities in our lives, so we should define life objectives for ourselves, plan for ourselves the best approach later on, and we will be more inspired to learn after the objectives are clear.

Contemplate any goals you need to accomplish:

There are certainly numerous things in life that we need to do, goals that we need to accomplish, and beliefs that we would especially prefer not to accomplish. To accomplish it, we need to concentrate hard.

Put forward attainable objectives:

Try not to define yourself a few objectives that you won't ever reach. That will just make yourself more visually impaired and incapable to begin. You can set yourself some present moment and simple to-accomplish objectives so you will be more persuaded to buckle down.

Stop cell phones and exhausting mingling:

Cell phones have essentially overwhelmed the existences of the vast majority, and exhausting social associations are turning out to be increasingly more unavoidable in our lives. Assuming we need to concentrate hard, we should stop cell phones and exhausting social connections and invest this energy considering.

CHAPTER THIRTY-FOUR

Inspirational Articles for Students to Getting Success : 2

Continue on in achieving your objectives.

Regardless you do, everything's about industriousness, regardless of how enormous or little it is. However long you persevere, you will acquire an alternate self. Learning is something very similar. Regardless you learn, you should persevere.

Persistent reflection and nonstop improvement

Enduring in learning isn't in every case extremely difficult work, however to keep a mentality of learning in the constant battle. We should proceed to reflect and keep on rousing ourselves to contemplate more diligently.

"10 Iconic Persons Success Stories For Motivation"

Articles About Student Motivation

To study and buckle down, It is nice to track down some rousing and Motivational articles for understudies. So what the understudies need to get inspiration for progress. How about we investigate.

Assurance

This is the factor that gives the most noteworthy scores to successful understudies. From this, we can likewise see their demeanor towards the school. The fundamental inspiration of the greater part of them doesn't come from outside factors, like forceful guardians and educators, or they are very shrewd and underestimate everything.

Interest

Most talented understudies accomplish something other than grades, they truly care about what they realize. Be interested about the world. It is a craving to get things. Accept me as an illustration I read a wide range of books ravenously. Wikipedia is my number one site. On the off chance that I don't continue to contemplate, I will feel exhausted and miserable.

Self pressing factor

Like assurance, this high score factor mirrors the understudies' longing for progress. It positions a lot higher than outside variables, for example, guardians and companion pressure.

Expectations

This is additionally a factor that scores very high. In spite of the fact that it is like assurance, aspiration is more centered around the eventual outcome than the present. For some, gifted understudies, getting high scores is significant on the grounds that it assists them with pursueing their professions and accomplish individual objectives.

CHAPTER THIRTY-FIVE

INSPIRATIONAL ARTICLES FOR STUDENTS TO GETTING SUCCESS : 3

Resourcefulness

Alright! Nobody says that insight isn't significant, yet it is undeniably less significant than elements like assurance and difficult work. The fact is that you don't need to be a virtuoso to perform well in school; most talented understudies additionally need to concentrate hard to accomplish their present accomplishments.

Family support and parental pressing factor

Gifted understudies rank the help of their families higher than their folks who consistently request that they get A. In my review, by far most of individuals (around 3/4) said their folks support them. Just 18% said that getting passing marks was compelled by their folks, and 7% of guardians couldn't have cared less about their school execution.

Great educator

The study results show that great instructors are significant, yet they are not a critical factor for gifted understudies. It's incredible to have an educator move you and urge you to go hard and fast, however you can't depend on this. During the time spent contemplating, you might experience a couple of horrendous educators (I have met), so you ought to be ready to confront instructors of different characters.

Friend pressure

This doesn't appear to be a vital factor. It could be useful to have companions to challenge you and cause you to perform well, yet most skilled understudies don't think this is a fundamental task for progress. By and by, these outside factors appear to be less significant than the understudies' assurance to succeed.

A few understudies don't gain a lot of headway until in the wake of moving on from secondary school. Ponder the inspiration for gifted understudies in these colleges.

Significance of Motivation for Students

Inspiration is something you need to make a solid effort to keep up with for the duration of your life (persuasive articles for understudies). It won't show up for the time being, however a progressive, complex, and exceptionally interior cycle. Most talented understudies have something somewhere down in their souls that constrains them to succeed.

As I would see it, inspiration is positive or negative. Great inspiration comes from the longing to work on yourself and understand your latent capacity, for example,

1.Interest.

2.Invest heavily in your accomplishments.

3.I need to go full scale.

4.Accept that you can do extraordinary things with your diligent effort.

5.Have elevated requirements of yourself.

6.Attempt to accomplish pragmatic objectives for what's to come.

*All things considered, you should attempt to stay away from awful intentions, for example,

1.Need to be superior to other people.

2.Need to get acclaim from guardians and educators.

3.scared of disappointment.

4 "Step by step instructions to Avoid Negative Influences in Life"

5.On the off chance that you neglect to accomplish your objective, you will feel remorseful or feel exceptionally pointless.

6.Attempt to accomplish restricted objectives with low achievement rates, like turning into the primary alumni or entering Yale Law School.

CHAPTER THIRTY-SIX

"Counterfeit It Until You Become It"

It very well may be not difficult to see execution as a single direction road. We regularly catch wind of a genuinely gifted competitor who fails to meet expectations on the field or a savvy understudy who struggles in the homeroom. The commonplace account about underachievers is that on the off chance that they could just "get their head right" and create the right "mental disposition" then, at that point they would perform in their prime.

There is no question that your mentality and your exhibition are associated somehow or another. Yet, this association works both ways. A sure and positive mentality can be both the reason for your activities and the aftereffect of them. The connection between actual execution and mental disposition is a two-way road.

Certainty is regularly the consequence of showing your capacity. This is the reason Garry Kasparov's technique for playing as though he felt sure could prompt real certainty. Kasparov was allowing his activities to rouse his convictions.

These aren't simply feel-acceptable thoughts or fleecy self improvement thoughts. There is hard science demonstrating the connection among conduct and certainty. Amy Cuddy, a Harvard specialist who studies non-verbal communication, has displayed through her earth shattering examination that essentially remaining in more certain postures can expand certainty and reduction nervousness.

Cuddy's exploration subjects experienced genuine organic changes in their chemical creation including expanded testosterone levels (which is connected to certainty) and diminished cortisol levels (which is connected to pressure and tension). These discoveries go past the well known phony it until you make it reasoning. As per Cuddy, you can "Fake it until you become it."

CHAPTER THIRTY-SEVEN

STEP BY STEP INSTRUCTIONS TO BUILD CONFIDENCE

Garry Kasparov and his long-lasting adversary Anatoly Karpov—two of the best chess players ever—took their separate seats around the chess board. The 1990 World Chess Championship was going to start.

The two men would play 24 games to choose the hero with the most noteworthy scoring player being announced the World Chess Champion. Altogether, the match would extend for 90 days with the initial 12 games occurring in New York and the last 12 games being played in Lyon, France.

Kasparov got going admirably, yet before long started to commit errors. He lost the seventh game and let various triumphs get away during the primary portion of the competition. After the initial 12 games, the two men left New York with the match tied at 6-6. The New York Times announced that "Mr. Kasparov had lost certainty and developed anxious in New York."

In case Kasparov planned to hold his title as the best on the planet, it planned to take all that he had.

"Playing Kasparov Chess"

Josh Waitzkin was a chess wonder as a youngster and won different U.S. Junior Championships before the age of 10. En route, Waitzkin and his dad had the chance to associate with Garry Kasparov and examine chess methodology with him. Specifically, they figured out how Kasparov managed astoundingly troublesome matches like the one he looked against Karpov in the 1990 World Chess Championship.

Kasparov was a savagely forceful chess player who blossomed with energy and certainty. My dad composed a book called Mortal Games about Garry, and during the years encompassing the 1990 Kasparov-Karpov match, we both invested a considerable amount of energy with him.

At a certain point, after Kasparov had lost a major event and was feeling dull and delicate, my dad asked Garry how he would deal with his absence of trust in the following game. Garry reacted that he would attempt to play the chess moves that he would have played in case he were feeling certain. He would profess to feel sure, and ideally trigger the state.

Kasparov was an intimidator over the board. Everybody in the chess world feared Garry and he benefited from that reality. In the event that Garry shuddered at the chessboard, adversaries would shrivel. So in case Garry was feeling terrible, yet puffed up his chest, taken forceful actions, and gave off an impression of being simply the sign of Confidence, then, at that point adversaries would become disrupted. Bit by bit, Garry would take care of off his own chess moves, off the made position, and off his adversary's structure dread, until soon enough the certainty would turn out to be genuine and Garry would be in stream...

He was not being fake. Garry was setting off his zone by playing Kasparov chess.

second half:

At the point when the second 50% of the World Chess Championship started in Lyon, France, Kasparov constrained himself to play forceful. He started to lead the pack by dominating the sixteenth match. With his certainty building, he ran through definitive successes in the eighteenth and twentieth games too. No matter what, Kasparov lost just two of the last 12 games and held his title as World Chess Champion.

He would keep on holding the title for an additional 10 years.

CHAPTER THIRTY-EIGHT

MEASURE YOUR PROGRESS

Assuming you need to figure out how to remain inspired to arrive at your objectives, then, at that point there is a second piece of the inspiration puzzle that is significant to comprehend. It has to do with accomplishing that ideal mix of difficult work and joy.

Chipping away at difficulties of an ideal degree of trouble has been found to not exclusively be persuading, yet in addition to be a significant wellspring of joy. As analyst Gilbert Brim put it, "One of the significant wellsprings of human satisfaction is dealing with undertakings at a reasonable degree of trouble, neither too hard nor excessively simple."

This mix of bliss and pinnacle execution is at times alluded to as stream, which is the thing that competitors and entertainers experience when they are "in the zone." Flow is the psychological state you experience when you are so centered around the main job that the remainder of the world disappears.

To arrive at this condition of pinnacle execution, be that as it may, you not just need to chip away at challenges at the right level of trouble, yet in addition measure your quick advancement. As therapist Jonathan Haidt clarifies, one of the keys to arriving at a stream state is that "you get quick input about how you are getting along at each progression."

Seeing yourself make improvement at the time is amazingly propelling. Steve Martin would make a wisecrack and promptly know whether it worked dependent on the giggling of the group. Envision how irresistible it is make a thunder of giggling. The surge of positive input Martin experienced from one incredible joke would likely be sufficient to overwhelm his feelings of dread and motivate him to work for quite a long time.

In different everyday issues, estimation appears to be unique yet is similarly as basic for accomplishing a mix of inspiration and satisfaction. In tennis, you get prompt criticism dependent on whether you win the point. Notwithstanding how it is estimated, the human cerebrum needs some approach to envision our advancement in case we are to keep up with inspiration. We should have the option to see our successes.

CHAPTER THIRTY-NINE

THE GOLDILOCKS RULE

The human mind adores a test, however just in case it is inside an ideal zone of trouble. In the event that you love tennis and attempt to play a genuine match against a four-year-old, you will immediately become exhausted. It's excessively simple. You'll win each point. Interestingly, in the event that you play an expert tennis player like Roger Federer or Serena Williams, you will rapidly lose inspiration in light of the fact that the match is excessively troublesome.

Presently consider playing tennis against a your equivalent. person. As the game advances, you win a couple of focuses and you lose a couple. You have a decent shot at winning, yet just in the event that you sincerely attempt. Your center river, interruptions disappear, and you end up completely put resources into the job needing to be done. This is a test of simply sensible trouble and it is a great representation of the Goldilocks Rule.

The Goldilocks Rule expresses that people experience top inspiration when working on undertakings that are directly on the edge of their present capacities. Not very hard. Not very simple. On the money.

Martin's satire profession is a magnificent illustration of the Goldilocks Rule practically speaking. Every year, he extended his satire schedule—however simply by a little while. He was continually adding new material, yet he additionally kept a couple of jokes that were ensured to get snickers. There were barely enough triumphs to keep him spurred and barely enough slip-ups to keep him buckling down.

CHAPTER FORTY

STEP BY STEP INSTRUCTIONS TO REMAIN PROPELLED

I as of late completed Steve Martin's superb collection of memoirs, Born Standing Up.

Martin's story offers a captivating point of view on the stuff to stay with propensities for the since a long time ago run. Satire isn't for the shy. It is difficult to envision a circumstance that would strike dread into the hearts of a larger number of individuals than performing alone in front of an audience and neglecting to get a solitary giggle. But Steve Martin confronted this dread each week for a very long time. As would be natural for him, "10 years went through learning, 4 years went through refining, and 4 years as a wild achievement."

Can any anyone explain why a few group, similar to Martin, stay with their propensities—regardless of whether rehearsing jokes or drawing kid's shows or playing guitar—while the majority of us battle to remain inspired? How would we configuration propensities that pull us in instead of ones that disappear? Researchers have been reading this inquiry for a long time. While there is still a lot to learn, perhaps the most reliable discoveries is that the best approach to keep up with inspiration and accomplish top degrees of want is to chip away at errands of "simply sensible trouble."

CHAPTER FORTY-ONE

Remain Motivated in Life and Business

In 1955, Disneyland had quite recently opened in Anaheim, California, when a ten-year-old kid strolled in and requested a task. Work laws were free in those days and the kid figured out how to land a position selling manuals for $0.50 each.

Inside a year, he had changed to Disney's sorcery shop, where he took in stunts from the more established representatives. He tried different things with jokes and evaluated straightforward schedules on guests. Before long he found that what he cherished was not performing wizardry yet acting overall. He put his focus on turning into a joke artist.

Starting in his adolescent years, he began acting in little clubs around Los Angeles. The groups were little and his demonstration was short. He was once in a while in front of an audience for over five minutes. A large portion of individuals in the group were too bustling drinking or chatting with companions to focus. One evening, he in a real sense conveyed his stand-up daily schedule to an unfilled club.

It wasn't charming work, however there was no question he was improving. His first schedules would just last a couple of minutes.

By secondary school, his material had extended to incorporate a five-minute demonstration and, a couple of years after the fact, a ten-minute show. At nineteen, he was performing week by week for twenty minutes all at once. He needed to peruse three sonnets during the show just to make the routine long enough, yet his abilities kept on advancing.

He went through one more decade testing, changing, and rehearsing. He accepted a position as a TV essayist and, progressively, he had the option to land his own appearances on television shows. By the mid-1970s, he had worked his direction into being an ordinary visitor on The Tonight Show and Saturday Night Live.

At last, after almost fifteen years of work, the youngster rose to acclaim. He visited sixty urban areas in 63 days. Then, at that point 72 urban areas in eighty days. Then, at that point 85 urban communities in ninety days. He had 18,695 individuals go to one show in Ohio. Another 45,000 tickets were sold for his three-day show in New York. He launch to the highest point of his class and became quite possibly the best joke artists of his time.

His name is Steve Martin.

CHAPTER FORTY-TWO

Four Tips For Boosting Exercise Motivation In Seniors

You're never too old to even consider creating or refine an activity program. Furthermore, there has never been greater freedom to discover a variety of projects that suit your inclinations, your wellness capacity and your lifestyle.As a more established grown-up, the explanations behind practice change: benefits incorporate assisting with controlling persistent conditions like hypertension and diabetes, fortifying muscles to forestall falls, and further developing adaptability to keep up with exercises of day by day living.An added advantage? Normal exercise can assist with boosting your temperament and work on your general feeling of prosperity. What's more, you'll make new companions! (Obviously, consistently converse with your primary care physician prior to beginning any sort of activity program.)Where to search for another activity program? Start with your neighborhood wellness or public venue. The key is discovering exercises that you appreciate. A few hints to begin:- Follow your inclinations. Like to move? Swim? Perhaps yoga or Tai-Chi sounds engaging. There are wellness classes for each taste and capacity level.- Follow your companions. Going to a wellness class with a companion works on your inspiration and in case you're going it single-handedly – here's your opportunity to make new companions!- Listen to your body. Exercise shouldn't be difficult to be helpful. Begin moderate and progress once again time.- Set objectives. How regularly would you like to work out?

How hard? Foster a three-to half year plan so you can quantify your success. But stand by, there's more: Older grown-ups who take an interest in bunch practice programs report worked on personal satisfaction from the social part of gathering wellness. The gathering makes a feeling of local area that helps keep you motivated. Social seclusion, which frequently prompts dejection, is normal among seniors, yet taking a wellness class can fashion a bond that keeps individuals returning for exercise and stretches out to associating outside of class. In a new investigation of grown-ups matured 65 years and more established, analysts overviewed 46,564 members in the SilverSneakers work out regime somewhere in the range of 2010 and 2016 to decide how exercise worked on their nature of life. "Even however ordinary actual work is significant, prosperity is about something other than work out," as indicated by Julie Logue, Training Manager at Tivity Health. "Through SilverSneakers, you can investigate a wide range of work out regimes, socialization and sustenance projects to help you carry on with your best life. We engage individuals to live better, more joyful, longer. "Older grown-ups with more continuous visits to wellness focuses who take an interest in SilverSneakers practice programs report altogether less days when they felt truly or intellectually unwell and appraised their physical and psychological well-being higher than the individuals who partook less oftentimes

15 Life Changing Points

1.Normal Doesn't Mean Secure. Since it's not unexpected, that doesn't mean it's not dangerous. Numerous individuals fall into the misguided judgment that if a many individuals are accomplishing something, it should be the most secure way.

2.Walk Slowly So You Don't Trip. The additional time you offer yourself to finish an objective, the almost certain you'll accomplish it. By embraced new objectives with intentional gradualness, you increment the possibility you can make enduring progress.

3.Instructions to Discover What You're Passionate About. Appreciating playing computer games isn't equivalent to burning through very long time planning your own. Your enthusiasm must be something you would buckle down for. So what do you do, in case there isn't anything you feel that connected about?

4.How Do You Want to Manage Your Life? How would you like to manage your life? It's an inquiry nearly everybody pose to themselves. It's additionally an inquiry I don't really accept that you should try asking in any case.

The Zen of Folding Laundry, and Other Thoughts on Happiness. Instructions to quit opposing life and acknowledge things.

5.Defeating the Frustration Barrier. When is the last time you went partner dancing, delivered a discourse, taken in another dialect, took up karate or even prepared another extraordinary food? When was the last time you accomplished something out of your usual range of familiarity?

6.YouSuck. Get Over It. Life is definitely not a consistent lift. At times improving necessitates that you initially deteriorate. In the event that you can't concede to yourself that you suck at something, odds are it will keep you away from future upgrades.

7.Walk Your Talk... One Step at a Time. Defects are important forever. I believe it's miserable that a few group feel that on the grounds that being completely steady with your qualities is unthinkable, that there is no point attempting to troubleshoot the irregularities.

8.Arete: The Meaning of Life. Arete is an antiquated Greek word meaning greatness or excellence. Utilizing arete as a standard for carrying on with life implies that you are centered around the nature of all that you do and experience.

9.The Laziest Solution Possible. Sluggishness is a decently underestimated ideals. It's equivalent word made the short rundown of dangerous sins (sloth) and it is normal seen as the significant guilty party behind an absence of accomplishment (he's keen yet he needs discipline). I end up intuition the inverse.

10.The most effective method to Not Want Things and Still Be Happy. Zero in on the cycle to remain glad, in any event, when you don't get what you need.

11.Be Ambitious With Goals, Not Deadlines. I've generally discovered that assuming you need to know what amount of time something will require, ask somebody who has effectively done it. Sounds self-evident, yet couple of individuals do it.

12.Irritated Chair Motivation. I think this rule is valid for a ton of things: when everything is going consummately, less things complete.

13.Keeping away from Motivation Burnout. You don't begin a long distance race by running the primary mile. So why attempt to run your life that way?

14.Request What You Want. The key explanation certainty is so amazing and attractive is basic, sure individuals request what they need.

15.In case You Aren't Getting Hate Mail, Your Writing Probably Sucks. It's just the thoughts that are new, imply dangers or push limits that get disdain mail. Those are likewise the thoughts that change the world.

24 Quotes About The Value Of Endlessly Using Time Effectively : 1

A second gone never returns.

We ought to comprehend the worth of time until it is past the point of no return. All things considered, it is forever our decision to utilize our time admirably or squander it in any case.

Do you Value your Time?

Everybody has a few dreams throughout everyday life. Dreams request time and exertion. We figure we will have a lot of time later to get things done.

Afterward, we understand that if we would do it prior, it might have been something more. Why it happens that we comprehend the worth of time when we lost it.

Here is the thing that extraordinary individuals say about the worth of time:

"Until you esteem yourself, you will not esteem your time. Until you esteem your time, you will do nothing with it." ~ M. Scott Peck

"The key is in not investing energy, however in contributing it." ~ Stephen R. Flock

"My #1 things in life don't cost any cash. Plainly the most valuable asset we as a whole have is time." ~ Steve Jobs

"Know the genuine worth of time; grab, seize, and partake in each snapshot of it." ~ Lord Chesterfield

"I suggest you deal with the minutes and the hours will deal with themselves." ~ Earl of Chesterfield

"Understand that now, at this time of time, you are making. You are making your next second. That is the thing that's genuine." ~ Sara Paddison

How we Spend our Time:

Check yourself. How you go through your day? It is safe to say that you are simply becoming mixed up in your every day exercises? Is it accurate to say that you are drawing near to your objectives throughout everyday life? Regularly we suspect as much however never figure out how to get it going.

Does cynicism gobble up your time? Now and again we center around the negative angle more than the positive. Negative deduction attempts to keep you at a similar spot.

Shift your concentration from "What is impossible" to "What should be possible". Invest your energy to push ahead throughout everyday life.

Allow us to see a few statements about the investing our energy admirably:

"In the event that you invest a lot of energy contemplating a thing, you'll never complete it." ~ Bruce Lee

"A great many people invest additional time and energy circumventing issues than in attempting to settle them." ~ Henry Ford

"Try not to invest energy beating on a divider, wanting to change it into an entryway." ~ Coco Chanel

"Customary individuals consider simply investing energy. Incredible individuals consider utilizing it." ~ Author Unknown

"Time is the thing that we need most, yet what we utilize most noticeably terrible." ~ William Penn

Do you set out to Waste your Time?

In the event that you think you are fooling around, you are incorrect here. In reality, time is squandering you step by step. Use yourself however much you can.

Here is the thing that they say about with nothing to do:

"Men discuss killing time, while time discreetly kills them." ~ Dion Boucicault

24 Quotes About The Value Of Endlessly Using Time Effectively : 2

"Dost thou love life? Then, at that point don't waste time, for that is the stuff life is made of." ~ Benjamin Franklin

"Time = Life, Therefore, burn through your time and misuse of your life, or expert your time and expert your life." ~ Alan Lakein

"Lost time is never found again." ~ Benjamin Franklin

"You can't get the ball really rolling. You can just improve later on." ~ Ashley Ormon

I don't have Time:

We generally whine about the absence of time. We as a whole have equivalent 24 hours and we can do a ton in those 24 hours. It is about needs.

Regularly we invest a great deal of energy on the things that are of less need like sitting in front of the TV, tattling, understanding paper and strolling to a great extent.

It is great to set aside a few minutes for happiness. Be that as it may, deal with your chance to chip away at the significant things too. You will consistently figure out how to do things that you truly need to do throughout everyday life.

Here are incredible platitudes for you on the off chance that you say you don't have time:

"Absence of heading, not absence of time, is the issue. We as a whole have 24 hour days." ~ Zig Ziglar

"You won't ever figure out an ideal opportunity for anything. Assuming you need time you should make it." ~ Charles Buxton

"The pith of self-control is to do the significant thing as opposed to the earnest thing." ~ Barry Wernick.

Try not to Wait. Start it today:

Time is valuable. Time is restricted. Try not to stand by so long to do anything throughout everyday life.

I have seen individuals who hang tight for the ideal time. They delay until they have an unmistakable picture. They delay until they will have all assets. Persistence is acceptable however you can't stand by for eternity. In the event that you continue to hang tight for long, you will lament later.

Do you figure out how to deal with your fantasies? If not presently when?

That's the last straw. Venture out. Move somewhat regular. Test with where you are and what you have. Your vision will turn out to be clear when you make a move.

Posting a few statements that advise us to begin utilizing our time at the present time:

"Try not to pause. The time won't ever be perfect." ~ Napoleon Hill

"Preferable three hours too early over a moment past the point of no return." ~ William Shakespeare

"Decide never to be inactive. No individual will have event to grumble of the need of time who never loses any. It is brilliant what amount should be possible in case we are continually doing." ~ Thomas Jefferson

"The best an ideal opportunity to plant a tree is twenty years prior. The subsequent best time is presently." ~ Proverb

"Each day in turn this is sufficient. Try not to think back and lament over the past for it is gone; and don't be pained about the future, for it has not yet come. Embrace current circumstances, and work everything out such that wonderful it will merit recollecting." ~ Unknown

Printed by Libri Plureos GmbH in Hamburg,
Germany